Ancient Sacred Sites in the Gulf of Naples
The Sanctuary of Athena at Punta Campanella

The geographical position between the gulfs of Naples and Salerno made pre-Roman Sorrento a fundamental point of passage. Around the inhabited centre, sacred sites or scattered settlements developed, including the sanctuary of Athena on the extreme tip of the peninsula near Punta Campanella. This book explores the historical development of the sanctuary from the 6th century BC to the 1st century AD. Drawing on partly unpublished archaeological documentation and literary sources, the book provides useful elements for understanding the site and its relationship with the surrounding area. Sorrento and the Greek presence in the Gulf of Naples are linked to the sanctuary installation, perhaps first dedicated to the Sirens but surely after to Athena. Judging from literary sources, it was one of the best-known places of worship in ancient Italy. It was only in the 1980s that the discovery of an Oscan inscription with a dedication to Minerva made it possible to hypothesise the presence of a sanctuary near the Medieval tower at Punta Campanella. The analysis of the archaeological documentation known until now, the study of the new archaeological plans and the material culture (ceramics) from the site make it possible to better understand the development and the importance of the sanctuary. This book, therefore, defines the historical and territorial development of the sanctuary of Athena, reconstructing the history of the territory of ancient Surrentum and, above all, its most important sanctuary. The book will be of particular interest to archaeologists, ancient historians and historians of religion.

Luca Di Franco is an archaeologist official of the Italian Ministry of Culture.

Young Feltrinelli Prize in the Moral Sciences
Roberto Antonelli
President, Class of Moral Sciences, Accademia Nazionale dei Lincei
Alberto Quadrio Curzio
President Emeritus, Accademia Nazionale dei Lincei
Alessandro Roncaglia
Joint Academic Administrator, Accademia Nazionale dei Lincei

The Accademia Nazionale dei Lincei, founded in 1603, is one of the oldest academies in the world. Since 2018 it has assigned four "Young Antonio Feltrinelli Prizes" every two years, directed to Italian researchers in the fields of moral sciences and humanities who are less than 40 years old. Each winner is then requested to write a book-length essay on their research and/or the perspectives of research in their field, directed to the general public. The Routledge Young Feltrinelli Prize in the Moral Sciences series thus includes high-quality essays by top young researchers, providing thoroughly readable contributions to different research fields. With this initiative, Accademia dei Lincei not only gives a remarkable grant to the winners of the prize in order to support their research activity, but also contributes to the international diffusion of the research of eminent young Italian scholars.

Petrarch and Boccaccio in the First Commentaries on Dante's *Commedia*
A Literary Canon Before its Official Birth
Luca Fiorentini

Pliny the Elder and the Matter of Memory
An Encyclopaedic Workshop
Anna Anguissola

Memory and Narrative at the origins of the Novel
Three studies, from Chrétien de Troyes to Proust
Lorenzo Mainini

Ancient Sacred Sites in the Gulf of Naples
The Sanctuary of Athena at Punta Campanella
Luca Di Franco

For more information about this series, please visit: www.routledge.com/Young-Feltrinelli-Prize-in-the-Moral-Sciences/book-series/YFP

Ancient Sacred Sites in the Gulf of Naples
The Sanctuary of Athena at Punta Campanella

Luca Di Franco

LONDON AND NEW YORK

First published 2024
by Routledge
4 Park Square, Milton Park, Abingdon, Oxon OX14 4RN

and by Routledge
605 Third Avenue, New York, NY 10158

Routledge is an imprint of the Taylor & Francis Group, an informa business

© 2024 Luca Di Franco

The right of Luca Di Franco to be identified as author of this work has been asserted in accordance with sections 77 and 78 of the Copyright, Designs and Patents Act 1988.

All rights reserved. No part of this book may be reprinted or reproduced or utilised in any form or by any electronic, mechanical, or other means, now known or hereafter invented, including photocopying and recording, or in any information storage or retrieval system, without permission in writing from the publishers.

Trademark notice: Product or corporate names may be trademarks or registered trademarks, and are used only for identification and explanation without intent to infringe.

British Library Cataloguing-in-Publication Data
A catalogue record for this book is available from the British Library

ISBN: 978-1-032-64753-1 (hbk)
ISBN: 978-1-032-64755-5 (pbk)
ISBN: 978-1-032-64754-8 (ebk)

DOI: 10.4324/9781032647548

Typeset in Times New Roman
by Apex CoVantage, LLC

Contents

About the author		*vi*
Acknowledgements		*vii*
Preface		*viii*
1	Introduction	1
2	History of the excavations and the research	6
3	The Sorrentine Peninsula based on archaeological sources	17
4	Access to the sanctuary: the Via Minervia	27
5	Punta Campanella: the archaeological record	35
6	Analysis of the context: the sanctuary of Athena	52
7	Chronological phases and clues to the nature of the cult	64
8	Conclusions	82
	Bibliography	*84*
	Index	*93*

About the author

Luca Di Franco is an archaeologist official for the Italian Ministry of Culture at the Soprintendenza Archeologia, Belle Arti e Paesaggio for the Naples Metropolitan Area, in charge of sites like Capri, Penisola Sorrentina and Piana Campana, and the scientific director of numerous archaeological excavations, including the Naples-Bari High Speed Railway. Previously in charge of the Roman section, archives and conservation of the collections at the National Archaeological Museum in Taranto and research assistant in Classical Archaeology at the University of Naples 'Federico II'. He is the author of scientific articles and monographs on sculptural productions from the Hellenistic-Roman period in Campania and central-southern Italy, on iconography and iconology in the classical world, on maritime villas from the Roman period and on the culture of antiquity. Most recently, he edited the international conference 'Le grotte tra Preistoria, età classica e Medioevo: Capri, la Campania, il Mediterraneo' ('Caves between Prehistory, the Classical Age and the Middle Ages: Capri, Campania, the Mediterranean'). He is scientific director of the 'Masgaba' project, concerning the study of antiquities on the island of Capri. He is the scientific director of, among others, the new excavations at Punta Campanella (sanctuary of Athena) and the villa of Gradola (Anacapri). He is the winner of the Antonio Feltrinelli Prize for archaeology, awarded in 2022 by the Accademia Nazionale dei Lincei.

Acknowledgements

This book comes from a long study and years of reflections. About three years ago, after becoming an archaeological official of the Sorrentine Peninsula, I visited Punta Campanella and saw the great potential of this ancient site extended towards the sea and marked by wars: the medieval tower, the Murattian batteries and the machine guns. Despite this, traces of the ancient sanctuary of Athena could still be seen. For this, I am indebted to teachings and encouragements that I must mention here in the introduction.

I owe sincere thanks to Teresa Elena Cinquantaquattro for advice and for sharing the new research on the Punta Campanella site; with her support, it was possible to plan and imagine new extensive excavations on the site. I am grateful to *Soprintendente* Mariano Nuzzo, who has now shared the importance of this research and has strongly wanted to enhance the site. My friend and special colleague Teresa Laudonia has always believed it possible to change the image we had of Punta Campanella, and together, thanks to her expertise on places and material culture, we have found a few traces of the sanctuary of Athena. A thought goes to my friend and colleague Francesca Mermati, who constantly stimulated my studies with very effective talks on sirens. Finally, I thank Sergio Fiorentino and Stefano Ruocco, strenuous protectors and lovers of the cultural heritage of Massa Lubrense.

My acknowledgment also goes to the many people who have supported me in the graphics, to Elena Russo, Gabriele Gomez de Ayala, Filomena Lucci, Alessandra Zurolo and Rossella Mazza: to them goes the credit for making possible the planning of the new excavations.

I also thank all those who have given me their advice and have re-read my text, and Emanuele Greco, Francesco D'Andria and Carlo Rescigno for discussions on the subject.

Preface

A long peninsula, mostly distinguished by a mountainous ridge, closes the Gulf of Naples to the south. It is characterised by a city located on a tuff plateau overlooking the sea, to which it gives its name: Sorrento, the ancient Surrentum. The geographical position between the gulfs of Naples and Salerno makes these places a fundamental point of passage. Around the inhabited centre, sacred sites or scattered settlements developed. They could constitute the limits of the ancient territory of pre-Roman Sorrento: on the one hand, on the heights of Piano, in the Trinità district, a necropolis and a sacellum, and on the other, the sanctuary of Athena on the extreme tip of the peninsula, near Punta Campanella. This land is full of mythical episodes: Ulysses is said to have founded the temple of Athena, and there is also a cult of the Sirens, also linked to the hero's mythical journey from Troy to Ithaca (Figure P.1).

Historical development, through the hitherto partly unpublished archaeological documentation and literary sources, can help to provide useful elements for understanding the area and its relationship with the surrounding area.

Sorrento and the Greek presence in the Gulf of Naples (Cumae and Neapolis) are linked to the sanctuary installation, first dedicated to the Sirens, hitherto unknown, and immediately after to Athena. Known from literary sources, it was one of the best-known places of worship in ancient Italy. It was only in the 1980s that the discovery of an Oscan inscription with a dedication to Minerva made it possible to hypothesise the presence of a sanctuary near the medieval tower at Punta Campanella. The analysis of the archaeological documentation known until now, the study of the new archaeological plans and the material culture (ceramics and choroplastic art) from the site make it possible to better understand the development and the importance of the sanctuary. The period investigated is from the 6th century BC to the 1st century AD.

The aim of the essay, therefore, is to define the historical and territorial development of the sanctuary of Athena, with the aim of reconstructing the history of the territory of ancient Surrentum and, above all, of its most important sanctuary.

Figure P.1 National Gallery of Victoria, Melbourne. J.W. Waterhouse, Ulysses and the Sirens (1891). Oil on canvas.

Credit: Google art project.

The book presented here constitutes an element of novelty with respect to current research: archaeological studies on the sanctuary of Punta Campanella had stopped since 1990 when Mario Russo's monograph was published in connection with the discovery of the Oscan inscription. Until now, the study of the evidence on the ground has remained substantially unpublished, and the analysis of the materials found on the site has been limited to the reconnaissance carried out by Russo himself and not to the analysis of the only real excavation carried out in 1987.

The study presented offers the possibility of investigating the site from several points of view: from an architectural one, based on new plans, from that of the evidence of material culture, and finally, from a cultic point of view. It is precisely the cult that is the point of beginning and end: the entire study of the archaeological framework leads us to understand the cult dynamics within their socio-political context ranging from the 6th century BC to the 1st century AD.

It is also important to update the context examined in the light of the most recent discoveries: an important parallel is the extra-urban sanctuary of Athena near Castro, currently being excavated by Francesco D'Andria and which has been providing new information for the understanding of Greek sanctuaries in Magna Graecia.

1 Introduction

Since ancient times, whoever sails into the Gulf of Naples from the south must cross a natural threshold, a broad opening between high limestone cliffs: on one side, the heights of Monte Tiberio on the island of Capri; on the other, the promontory at the tip of the Sorrentine Peninsula, today known as Punta Campanella (Figures 1.1–1.5).

In Antiquity, this route was particularly important given that overland access to the plain of Naples and the Phlegraean Fields was obstructed to the west and south by high mountains, making the maritime approach the safest. The site of Punta Campanella (Figure 1.5)[1] was thus geographically strategic, and it is no coincidence that it hosted one of the most famous Greek sanctuaries dedicated to the goddess Athena.

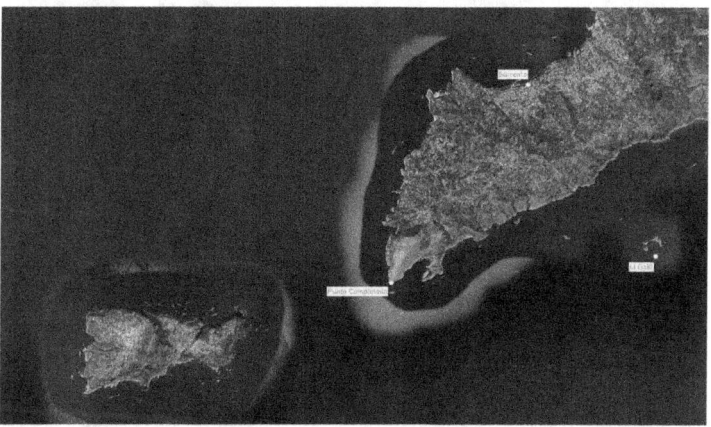

Figure 1.1 Satellite view of the Sorrentine Peninsula and Capri, showing Sorrento, Punta Campanella and the Li Galli islets.

Credit: Google Earth.

DOI: 10.4324/9781032647548-1

2 Introduction

Figure 1.2 View of Punta Campanella with Capri in the background.
Credit: Author.

Figure 1.3 3D model of Punta Campanella. View from the south.
Credit: Soprintendenza Archive.

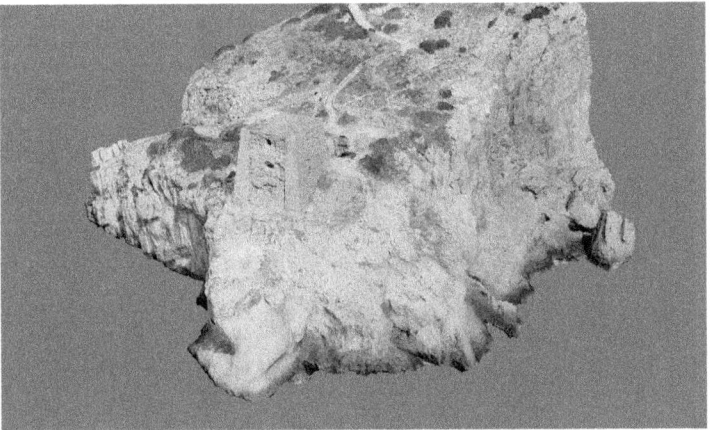

Figure 1.4 3D model of Punta Campanella. View from the west.
Credit: Soprintendenza Archive.

The ancient territory of Surrentum is also known to have hosted the cult of the Sirens, whose temple was considered by Timaeus of Locri to be one of the wonders of the West.[2]

According to the historian Diodorus Siculus[3], after Liparus, son of the king Ausonus, was driven out of Italy, taking refuge for a time on the island named after him, he conquered the territory of *Surrentum* with the help of his son-in-law Aiolos and ruled there until his death. However, the assumption – now known to be mistaken – that Surrentum had Greek origins derived from the sanctuaries located within the territory: that of the Sirens, mentioned by Strabo in two separate passages[4], and that of Athena, also mentioned by Strabo as well as Statius. Pliny the Elder, in contrast, speaks of a *promontorium Minervae*, once the seat of the Sirens.[5] At the height of the Roman period, the *liber coloniarum* stated that the land belonging to the temple of Athena was cultivated by the Greeks.[6] The *ager* of Surrentum was consecrated to Athena/Minerva, who thus may well also have been the polyadic goddess of the city.

In the 20th century, scholars began to examine the characteristics of the cults of Surrentum. Following the publication in 1946 of the surveys by Paolino Mingazzini and the discoveries of the 1980s made by Mario Russo, interest focused on the archaeological context of the ancient *athenaion acroterion* (Cape Athenaeum). The numerous investigations of this site over time make it possible to clarify the chronological and architectural development of the sanctuary with greater precision. In addition, analysis of the context can provide useful clues to the organisation of the cult in relation to the divinity

4 Introduction

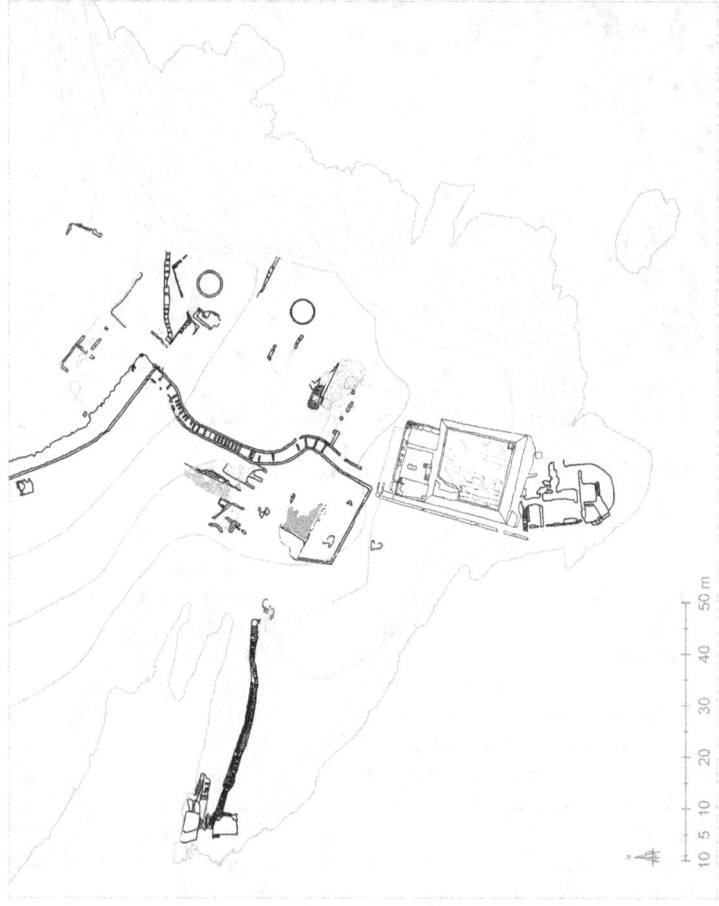

Figure 1.5 Site plan of Punta Campanella showing all ancient, medieval and modern structures.

Credit: Author.

or divinities but, above all, to the political arrangements with which it was associated. This book thus aims to provide an account of the archaeological investigations and discoveries in the area of Punta Campanella, a description of the surviving masonry structures, including a new site plan and floor plans, an analysis of the context and, lastly, the data that might help to reconstruct the cult.

Notes

1 Given the breadth of the bibliography, covered more specifically in the text, it seems useful to include here the main reference bibliography on Punta Campanella site: Capasso 1846; Beloch 1989, 310–314; Mingazzini, Pfister 1946, 17, 45–50, 51–53, 83–84; Russo 1990; *Campanella* 1992; De Caro 1992; Breglia Pulci Doria 1998; Leone 1998, 47–49 and *passim*; Caputo 2004, 84–87; Carafa 2008, 131–138; Adinolfi, Senatore 2015; Breglia 2016. The site plan presented here for the first time was produced through orthophotos of the whole area, supplemented by field measurements following partial vegetation clearing. The graphic elaboration was supported by Elena Russo under the coordination of Luca Di Franco: this is preparatory to the planning of the archaeological investigations, restorations and valorisation of the site financed by the Ministry of Culture and conducted by the Soprintendenza Archeologia, Belle Arti e Paesaggio for the Metropolitan Area of Naples under the scientific direction of Luca Di Franco.
2 Pseudo-Aristotle, *De mirab.*, 103.
3 D.S., V, 7.
4 Strab., I, 2, 12; V, 4, 8.
5 Plin., *Nat.* III, 61.
6 Lachmann, *Grom. vet.* I 236,22.

2 History of the excavations and the research[1]

Over time, the site of Punta Campanella has seen occasional discoveries and archaeological excavations which, when analysed with reference to modern graphic and photographic documentation and post-ancient history, make it possible to reconstruct the archaeological context fairly precisely (Figure 2.1).

After the inevitable decline of the area as a result of the fall of the Roman empire, fortifications and other structures for the defence of the territory were built on the site. In around 1334, during the Angevin period, a watchtower was built at the tip of the peninsula, although its current layout is the result of remodelling by the Aragonese.[2] The tower has played a fundamental role in the history of the site since the toponym is derived from it: when pirates or attackers were seen approaching by lookouts on the tower, a bell was rung. In the *Aestates surrentinae* published in 1696, Nicola Partenio Giannettasio records the presence on the promontory of mosaic paving but, above all, columns bearing capitals sculpted with little owls, sacred to Athena.[3] Similar observations were made a short time later by Filippo Anastasio in 1732[4] and his nephew, Ludovico Agnello Anastasio,[5] highlighting the presence of capitals and other marbles on the promontory. The presence of columns and other marbles was then confirmed by an excavation campaign designed to strip the site of pieces with which to embellish the church of San Vincenzo a Sorrento, later demolished to make room for Villa Tritone.[6] It was here that Umberto Pappalardo[7] noted a capital with the same features, which he identified with those described in previous centuries. Today, the piece is kept in the Museo Archeologico Territoriale della Penisola Sorrentina "G. Vallet" in Piano di Sorrento. There are indeed winged figures on the corners, but it is not clear whether these are little owls (Figure 2.2).

In the early 19th century, reflecting the location's strategic value, artillery batteries were installed on the two highest and flattest terraces by Joachim Murat. One of the walls delimiting and protecting the terrace had the effect, possibly deliberate, of blocking access to the flight of steps carved in the rock that led down to the so-called *approdo di levante* (Eastern Landing).

Also during the 19th century, in around 1850, on one of the rocky spurs below the Angevin tower, the first lighthouse was built. This was a two-storey

DOI: 10.4324/9781032647548-2

Figure 2.1 Punta Campanella. Late 19th century photo.
Credit: Archeoclub Massa Lubrense.

structure built to a rectangular plan (the dwelling of the lighthouse operator), from which a semicircular extension housing the light source (lantern) protruded towards the sea.

In 1890,[8] the observant and meticulous Karl Julius Beloch wrote that nothing remained of the temple at Punta Campanella. Indeed, he saw what he believed were the remains of a Roman villa with *opus signinum*, *opus reticulatum*, marbles and mosaics.

Shortly after the end of World War II, the Municipality of Massa Lubrense set up "*cantieri scuola*" (training building sites) in 1949 for measures that envisaged "repairs to the municipal road leading from Termini to Punta

8 History of the excavations and the research

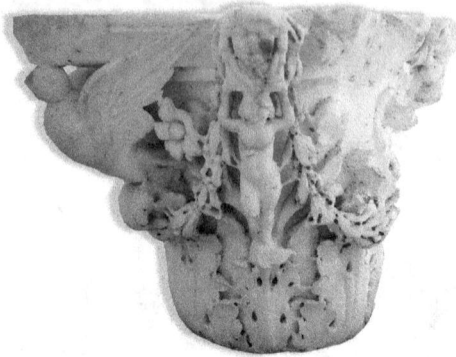

Figure 2.2 Piano di Sorrento, Museo Archeologico Territoriale della Penisola Sorrentina "G. Vallet". Capital perhaps found at Punta Campanella.

Credit: Author.

Campanella, damaged by wartime events".[9] It was in these circumstances that the paved road to the end of the peninsula was built, and since then, it has been modernised and restored many times.[10]

A key development was the work of Paolino Mingazzini and Friederich Pfister in 1946. With the help of the surveyor, the archaeologist provided the first ever complete picture of the visible structures (Figure 2.3), which they mostly identified as corresponding to a Roman villa.

Such a building is hinted at in the literary sources, which speak of a structure that needed to be ready at all times for the emperor Tiberius, living in self-imposed exile on the nearby island of Capri.[11]

On the morning of 6 August 1969, as a result of a fire, the lighthouse operator's house was destroyed by an explosion, together with the light. It thus became necessary to build a new house for the lighthouse operator north of the Angevin tower and a new pylon for the beacon, which is still in use today. The rebuilt lighthouse operator's house has recently been demolished, although traces of the foundations remain.

The 1960s saw the first archaeological investigations at the site: in 1966, 1968 and 1978, Jean-Paul Morel conducted non-systematic collections of material sporadically distributed on the surface between the Bay of Ieranto and Punta Campanella, amounting to more than 700 ceramic fragments.[12] The author dated the material to the period from the third quarter of the 6th century BC to the first half of the 1st century AD, the specimens of Aretine ware attesting in his view to the villa's Tiberian phase.[13] For the first time, Morel offered a clear chronological account of the classes of material present, providing a solid basis for subsequent studies,[14] as well as suggesting that the votive deposits were located near the tower, near which most of the fragments were recovered.[15]

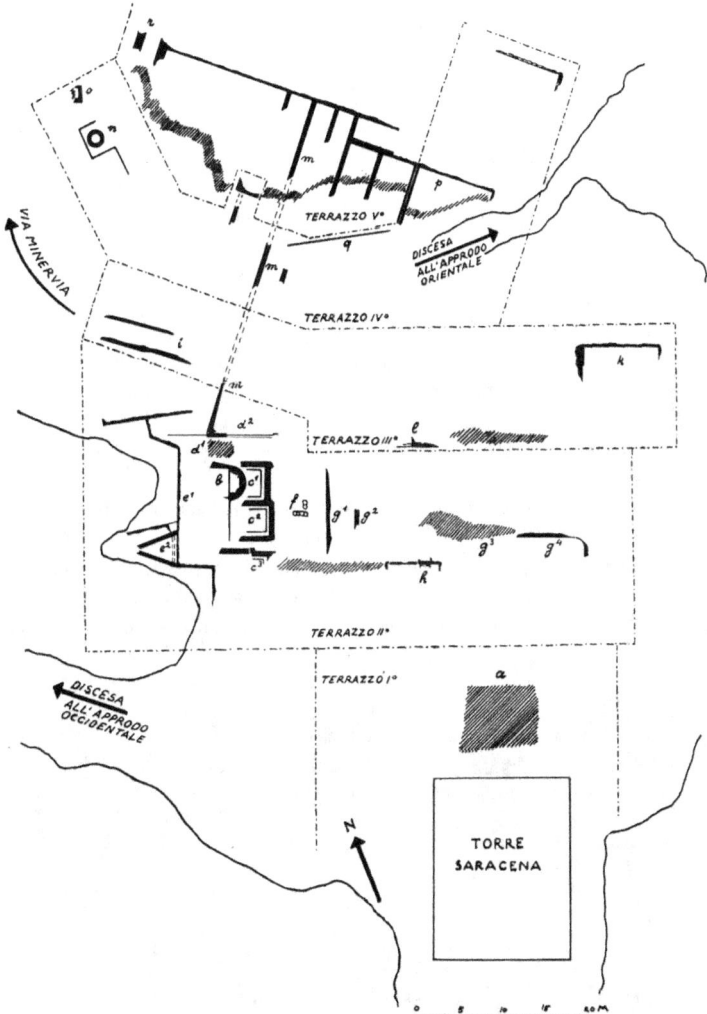

Figure 2.3 Site plan of Punta Campanella according to Paolino Mingazzini.
Credit: Soprintendenza Archive.

Between 1977 and 1979, various reconnaissance operations in the archaeological area, specifically north of the tower between the pylon and the western steps, led to the discovery of an initial nucleus of 375 fragments.[16] Following further reconnaissance, between 1979 and 1984, approximately 7,500 more finds were discovered on the north side of the tower, in the cellar of the tower and on the first two terraces. Among these were the ceramic classes already identified by Morel.[17]

On 17 November 1981, precisely as a result of this initial research and the floor plans drawn up by Paolino Mingazzini, an archaeological protection order was drawn up on the basis of Italian law 1089/39 and signed by the *Soprintendente* (Superintendent for Archaeological Heritage) Fausto Zevi. However, the site had already been declared an area of archaeological interest in 1969, as shown by protocol note 3050 of 18 March, signed by *Soprintendente* Alfonso de Franciscis.[18]

The most striking discovery took place in 1985, when Aniello Coppola identified an inscription carved in the rock along the steps on the Ieranto side. The presence of the inscription was reported to Mario Russo, who found that it was a text in Oscan, making it possible to identify the location of the sanctuary of Athena for the first time. The discovery, initially included in the acts of the Conference on Magna Graecia of 1985, is extensively analysed in the famous volume edited by Mario Russo and published by the *Accademia Nazionale dei Lincei* in 1990.[19]

The first systematic excavation at Punta Campanella took place from 2 to 22 August 1987. Conducted as an educational project, it was headed by Valeria Sampaolo, an official employed by the *Soprintendenza Archeologica* (archaeological authority) of Naples.[20] The excavation focused on the lowest terrace of the promontory (Figure 2.4) and entailed clearing the area,

Figure 2.4 Punta Campanella. Soprintendenza investigations in 1987. View of the western sector.

Credit: Soprintendenza Archive.

removing vegetation and alluvial soils from around the masonry remains and conducting a graphic and photographic survey of the entire flat area north of the tower (Figures 2.5–2.7).

The operations also involved the removal of material from the collapsed terminal stretch of the *Via Minervia*, which was documented for the first time on this occasion, about 12 m being brought to light. Two symmetrical flights of steps joining this terrace with the one above also emerged. The circular structure on the downhill side of the modern road to the north-east, the so-called *specula* according to Mingazzini, was also subject to clean-up and the removal of vegetation. In the course of these operations, a few thousand finds, to which we shall return, were discovered.

Of fundamental importance in the history of the studies is the previously mentioned work by Mario Russo, in which, for the first time since Morel, complementing the discussion of the rock-cut epigraph, the materials recovered by the author himself in the course of the reconnaissance, together with others held in private collections,[21] were carefully analysed.[22] The author himself returned to the theme in 1992 with the publication of new data arising from reconnaissance near the tower.[23]

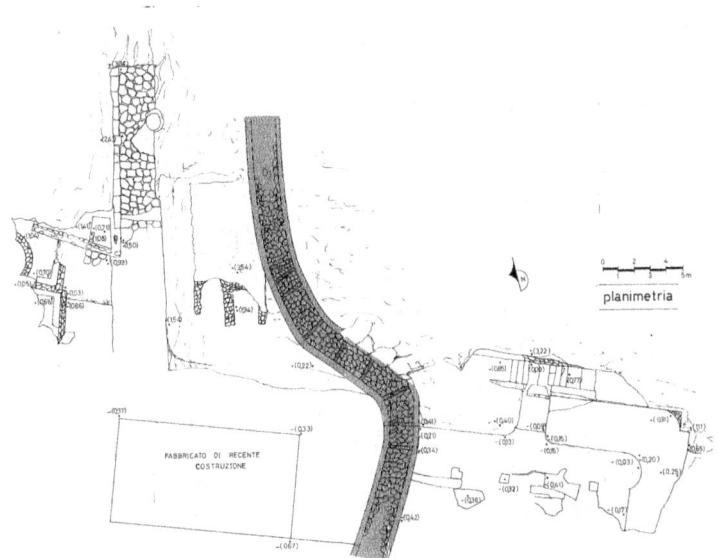

Figure 2.5 Punta Campanella. Soprintendenza investigations in 1987. General site plan of the excavations.

Credit: Soprintendenza Archive.

12 History of the excavations and the research

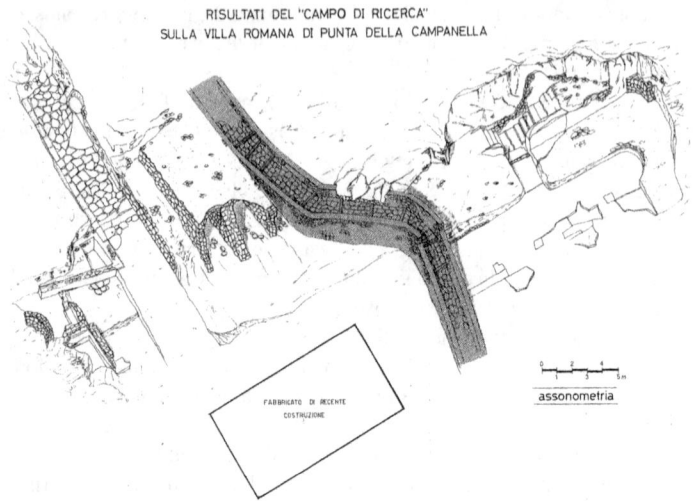

Figure 2.6 Punta Campanella. Soprintendenza investigations in 1987. General axonometry of the excavations.

Credit: Soprintendenza Archive.

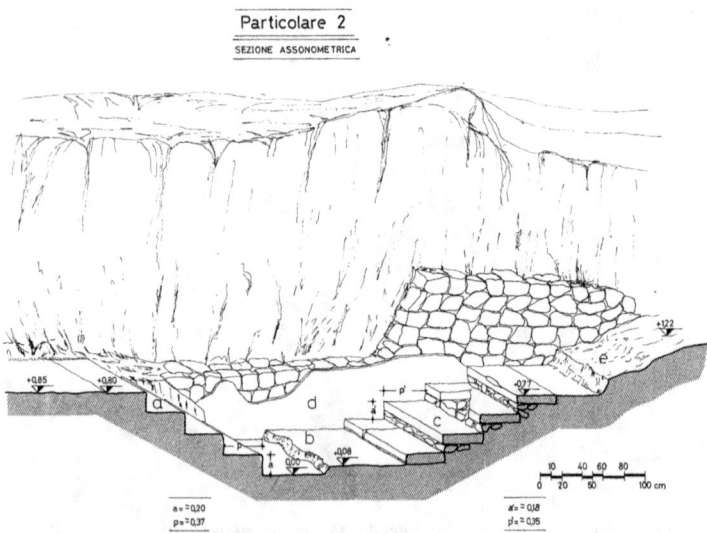

Figure 2.7 Punta Campanella. Soprintendenza investigations in 1987. Axonometry of the flight of steps carved in the rock.

Credit: Soprintendenza Archive.

The chronological framework presented by Russo was slightly higher than the one proposed by Morel, with the most ancient materials dated to the first quarter of the 6th century BC. As well as a broader and more precise presentation of the classes of materials,[24] greater emphasis is placed on coroplastic art.[25] The typological classification provided by the author, the images of Athena and the numerous female figures still form the basis of recent studies of the theme, which generally concur in seeing the adoption of similar models in the sanctuaries of nearby Stabiae and Pompeii.[26] In 1992, the discussion of classes became more detailed, with the addition of a fragment of *impasto* pottery and some fragments of carinated bowls in *bucchero*, which, together with the Ionic bowls of the B2 type and other ceramics in the Ionic tradition, represented the most ancient materials found in the area.[27]

From July to September 1990, at the behest of the *Soprintendenza Archeologica*, three archaeological assays were conducted by Luciana Jacobelli, specifically one in the tower and two outside it, the account published in 1994. A study of the materials was not performed, but the results presented do not change the picture thus far delineated.

In 2003, control of the archaeological area of Punta Campanella passed from the Ministry of Defence to the Municipality of Massa Lubrense.[28] This development marked the start of operations to improve the accessibility of the site. In 2004, in the course of works to extend the electricity grid in the area by means of underground cables, numerous archaeological assays were conducted along Via Campanella in the stretch between Mitigliano and Cancello.

Also in 2004, two small assays were conducted in the area of the two artillery batteries built in the reign of Murat: discovered on the second terrace was a row of squared limestone blocks, oriented east-west, on which were the remains of the bases of two columns, presumably once connected to a building, and, on the uphill side, a threshold. In contrast, on the terrace above, walls of uncertain date were brought to light, probably serving to stabilise the terrace.

In 2015 and 2016, during work to repair and improve the modern access road, other important excavations were conducted along the *Via Minervia* in the stretch between the tower of Fossa Papa and the tower at Punta Campanella. The assays, carried out under the scientific direction of Tommasina Budetta by Carmelo Rizzo and Rosa Cannavacciuolo, brought to light stretches of the ancient road (Figure 2.8).[29]

Lastly, the summer of 2021 saw an initial attempt to clean up the masonry remains already recorded by Paolino Mingazzini, subject to partial excavation in 1987. The operation focused on the area of the so-called *specula*, the three terraces and the *Via Minervia* with its associated structures.

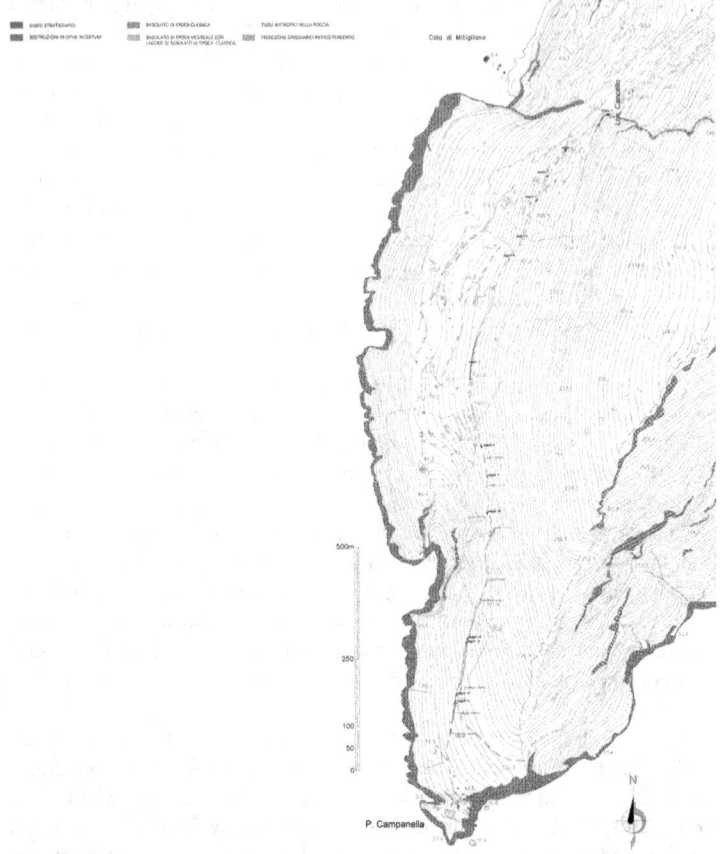

Figure 2.8 Massa Lubrense. Site plan of the excavations and the route of the ancient Via Minervia.

Credit: Soprintendenza Archive.

Notes

1 I owe sincere and affectionate thanks to the painstaking collection of documentation carried out by Stefano Ruocco, president of the Archeoclub of Massa Lubrense, from which this paragraph of the contribution was drawn. A summary of (modern) building interventions carried out at Punta Campanella is in Adinolfi, Senatore 2015, 322–332.
2 On the medieval tower, see Pollone, Romano 2015.
3 Giannettasio 1696, 2, 1722, 26.
4 Anastasio 1732, 250–251.
5 Anastasio 1751, 159.

History of the excavations and the research   15

6   Puglia 1995.
7   Pappalardo 1993, 68.
8   Beloch 1989, 313.
9   The report of this intervention bears the date 15 June 1949 and the signature of engineer Matteo Mosca. It describes in detail the precarious conditions in which the "mule track" road was in the postwar period. It then gives an account of how, in the years 1941, 1942 and 1943, in order to accommodate a number of military garrisons with related armaments (Artillery: 14° Reggimento, 274 Batteria Costiera, with howitzers of mm. 305 and mm. 149; units of the Genio Militare: 10° Reggimento Genio; units of Milizia: at the lighthouse of Punta Campanella; in addition, four antiaircraft observers had been arranged: one of the Milizia and three of the Artiglieria), the road had undergone incisive work in order to make it driveable, for which explosives were also used. When the war was over, after a few years, the road was again impassable, presenting heavily rutted. The report of Mosca, in addition to providing the previously mentioned news, describes the works to be done along the whole road of 3.580 km, which was divided into four sections: 1) A-B (from the Tower to Via Fosso La Papa) 1,000 ml.; 2) B-C (from Via Fosso La Papa to Canciello) 910 ml.; 3) C-D (from Canciello to Via Mitigliano) 710 ml.; 4) D-E (from via Mitigliano to Piazza Termini) 960 ml. (Municipality of Massa Lubrense Archive, n. 01236-L).
10 A second intervention, aimed at repairing the road following flood damage, affected only the initial section from Piazza Termini to the junction of Via Mitigliano (Municipality of Massa Lubrense Archive, n. 02820-L).
11 Mingazzini, Pfister 1946, 17, 45–50, 51–53, 83–84.
12 Morel 1982. A part of the objects are preserved at the Museo Archeologico Nazionale di Napoli in a suitcase.
13 Morel 1982. In the text, Morel clearly defines the chronological period of diffusion of the materials classes: he indicates, among the oldest, the Ionic bowls and some black-glaze specimens of Attic production, in addition to the Attic red-figure productions; more attention is given to the black-glaze pottery, which, together with the coroplastic art, locally produced red-figure vases, achromatic pottery and a particular production of local imitation *Saint-Valentain* vessels, are the most representative classes for the Hellenistic period of the sanctuary.
14 Although he does not provide quantitative data for each class, it is clear from the scholar's brief discussion how the Archaic period has the fewest testimonies, which increase overwhelmingly in the 4th-3rd century BC.
15 Morel 1982, 151.
16 Such objects were seen only in part by M. Russo and P. Zancani as recalled by the scholar in Russo's 1990 publication. See Russo 1990, 251, note 8.
17 These lists, at this stage of the research, are indicative only for objects quantification data, as they were not designed in chronological order nor according to material classes; however, the brief information given for each object or for groups of objects allows us to confirm the classes indicated by Morel and later by Russo: black and red-figure pottery, Attic and locally produced, black-glaze pottery, overpainted pottery, miniaturists, loom weights, ointmentaries and oil lamps.
18 The same *Soprintendente*, by note prot. 3049 of the same day, had also declared the stretch of road from Termini to Punta Campanella to be of important archaeological interest, cfr. Museo Archeologico Nazionale di Napoli, *Archivio Corrente*, M1/29.
19 Russo 1990.
20 Authorised by note prot. 20776 of 16 July 1987. The operations were conducted by archaeologist Margherita Tuccinardi, with surveying by architect Roberto Zanini of the national CTS of the Archeoclub.
21 Russo 1990, 9: Manniello collection and other private citizens; private collections at which materials from the Campanella are held also include the Fluss and Anastasio.

22 Russo 1990, 251: "Il materiale da me raccolto è costituito generalmente da residui lasciati da 'raschiatori' o scavatori clandestini che continuano a scavare buche nei cumuli di detriti originati dalle buche ben più profonde fatte per le batterie, per la costruzione del faro e della nuova casa del guardiano".
23 *Campanella* 1992. Presented here are 75 objects he recovered during a 1985 survey.
24 The framework of the classes presented in the 1990 work by M. Russo: votive coroplastic statuettes (including female heads and busts, with *polos* or crested helmet, paragnatids, shield resting on the left leg; standing female figures), Corinthian pottery, black-glaze pottery, Ionic-type pottery, the miniaturists, Attic black and red-figure pottery, the Italiot red-figure pottery, loom weights, fictile *louteria*, architectural terracottas as well as African terra sigillata and kitchen pottery.
25 Russo 1990, 72.
26 Russo 1990, 255; Miniero et al. 1997, 14; Miniero 2005; recently Parisi 2017, 192–194.
27 Russo 1992, 204–212. The study of the objects leads the author to an Etruscan-Italic reading of the sanctuary, especially on the basis of comparison with habitation and necropolis contexts from the Sorrento area to the Picentine countryside.
28 The transition from the Ministry of Defense to the Municipality of Massa Lubrense was neither simple nor without tension, as initially the site was put up for auction (see Museo Archeologico Nazionale di Napoli, *Archivio Corrente*, M14/1). To this phase dates the imposition of the historical-artistic constraint on the tower, ordered by Ministerial Decree of 5 August 1998.
29 Partially published work in Budetta, Cannavacciuolo, Rizzo 2018.

3 The Sorrentine Peninsula based on archaeological sources

To understand the importance of the site of Punta Campanella it is necessary to consider the sanctuary within the wider geographical and political context, which encompasses the city of *Surrentum*, its territory and the political power to which the sanctuary of Punta Campanella was subject.

The Sorrentine Peninsula – and its main urban settlement, Surrentum[1] – constituted a key territory in geographical and political terms in all its ancient phases of occupation. In addition, it was affected by environmental factors that, on the one hand, made it fertile terrain for the development of civilisations and settlements, and on the other, prompted their evolution and consequent adaptation. The sea, an element of both union and division, was also one of the few channels for communication given the geographical conformation of the territory, characterised by heights sloping steeply down to the sea, often unsuitable for urban settlement.[2] Another key feature of the landscape was Vesuvius, which represents the most unstable variable due to the continuous and constant evolution of the territory: the numerous eruptions over time, accompanied, preceded or followed by powerful earthquakes, shaped human occupation, affecting the perception of its ancient conformation over time.

The close connections between the peoples occupying this borderland territory are clear from an analysis of the literary sources. The pre-Roman population of the Sorrentine peninsula was broadly 'Ausonian', with a strong Etruscan influence stretching from the mouth of the Sele to the mouth of the Sarno, with the Etruscan Pontecagnano controlling the mouth of the Picentino, Fratte di Salerno the mouth of the Irno and Pompeii the mouth of the Sarno. North of the Gulf of Naples (*Kumaios kolpos*) in this period, there was a Greek presence, whose influence became dominant in the 6th century BC, culminating in the institution of the cult of the Sirens in the settlement of Cumae, later identified with Neapolis and the establishment of definitive control over the relative stretch of coastline. This century also saw the creation of the sanctuary of Punta Campanella, as we shall see dedicated to Athena.[3] The stratification of myths centred on primordial kingdoms can also be attributed to this period: in addition to Liparus, mentioned previously, there was Telon, king of the Teleboans, and Oebalus, his son, who ruled over Capri.[4] In the

DOI: 10.4324/9781032647548-3

6th century BC, Surrentum and Capri became crucial to commercial traffic, which the Greeks are believed to have dominated. The situation regarding the 4th century BC, when the conquest of the larger cities by the Samnites led to greater cultural uniformity, is a little clearer. Reflecting this complex stratification of peoples and cultural influences, Strabo claimed that in the Augustan period, Surrentum was Campanian,[5] while Stephanus of Byzantium stated that it was Etruscan.[6]

In archaeological terms, the development of coastal settlements can be read in this light: on the edge of the plain of the Sarno lies *Stabiae*, situated on the heights of Varano, whose conformation and layout are similar to those of Surrentum and other Campanian cities.[7] The earliest traces date the establishment of the settlement to the second half of the 7th century BC, with an intensification in the 6th century[8] followed by a decline in the 5th century and a new increase in the 4th century.

Another case is that of the small settlement of *Aequa* (Vico Equense), known for its necropoleis, whose urban layout can be hypothetically derived from the current old town, indicating that it was built in a defensive position on high ground overlooking the coast.[9] Here, too, the data from the necropoleis[10] point to occupation starting in the late 7th century BC and continuing uninterrupted until the Roman era, with significant attestations in the 5th and 4th centuries BC.

Near the tip of the peninsula, on a patch of high ground that straddles the ridge, not for nothing called Sant'Agata sui Due Golfi ("on the two gulfs"), in the Deserto district, a rich necropolis was discovered. Composed of a number of separate clusters, it was clearly associated with a settlement whose name is, however, unknown.[11] In this case, too, the corpses were buried in the ground, either in sarcophagi or in cavities lined and covered with slabs of tuff, dated to the period from the late 7th to the 5th centuries BC. To this necropolis must be attributed the tombs discovered on the Sorrento hills that were reported and described by Paola Zancani Montuoro,[12] one of which yielded a bowl with the term *Brandion* inscribed in the Euboean version of the Greek alphabet.

And so we come to the main city, Surrentum. Unfortunately, there are few literary sources, and they do not provide many details on the city's territorial reach in the pre-Roman period.[13] The most ancient traces of Surrentum are dated to the 7th and 6th centuries BC. They include the grave goods discovered near the Hotel Vittoria (Figure 3.1)[14] and those from Sottomonte that ended up in the Fluss collection, mentioned in Mingazzini's reports.[15]

The items are mainly from burials of inhumed individuals, deposed in sarcophagi or in cavities lined and covered with slabs of tuff and accompanied by rich grave goods. In the 6th century BC, what had probably been a rather scattered, low-density settlement took on a more definite urban character.[16] Situated on a tufaceous upland bordered by two valleys, the Vallone dei Mulini to the east and the Rio della Conca to the west, and the sea to the north, from

Figure 3.1 Sorrento, Museo Correale di Terranova. Bronze situla from the Hotel Vittoria necropolis.

Credit: Teresa Laudonia photograph.

which it was separated by a high cliff, it was easily defended and at the same time in direct contact with the sea.

The necropoleis developed all around it, and signs of its occupation, right up until the Roman period, are linked to funerary contexts. The necropoleis of Surrentum are believed to have been mainly located along the main access road, the *Via Minervia*, and around the urban perimeter. This explains why large clusters of burials, mostly Roman but with traces of earlier phases, were discovered along Corso Italia, in the Sottomonte district, near the Hotel Vittoria and along Via degli Aranci.

Other elements important for understanding pre-Roman Surrentum are the walls and the urban layout. The walls followed roughly the same course as the Aragonese circuit today, and the surviving gates, those of Parsano Nuovo and Marina Grande (Figure 3.2), are of ancient origin.

Figure 3.2 Sorrento, Porta Marina. Ancient gate in the north-west side of the wall circuit.

Credit: Author.

The other walls were, in contrast, located near the road leading to Marina Piccola, where the modern port is located, and to the east and west of the city. The latter, demolished in the late 19th century, marked the beginning and end of the *decumanus maximus*, itself the urban continuation of the *Via Minervia*. The other roads are perfectly conserved in the alignments of the modern buildings: three *decumani* are crossed by the *cardines*, with the *cardo maximus*, which ran along the eastern side of the Roman forum, corresponding to the modern Via Tasso. The surviving gates, in squared blocks of local tuff, the walls and the urban layout as a whole were established in the 4th and 3rd centuries BC and thus during the period of strong Oscan-Samnite influence.[17]

The material that emerges from these early phases of occupation points to a close connection between Surrentum and other sites on the Sorrentine Peninsula and between these and the Valley of the Sarno. Indeed, the same composition of grave goods is found in the necropolis of Sant'Agata sui

Due Golfi and that of Via Nicotera in Vico Equense. These two settlements seem to share a similar cultural horizon, which continued until the Hellenistic epoch when the Oscan-Samnite component seems to have been prevalent. The main link between them is Pompeii, whose political role under the aegis of the Etruscans is gradually being clarified by new studies.[18] Starting in the 6th century BC, and especially after the battle of Cumae in 474 BC, the Euboean Greek influence increasingly came to dominate the equilibria on the Sorrentine Peninsula, at least until the arrival of the Romans.

The discovery of numerous inscriptions in an Italic language with an alphabet described as Nucerian-Sorrentine indicates an Italic cultural substrate.[19] The pre-Roman Sorrentine Peninsula, and Surrentum in particular, thus played a fundamental role in bringing together different peoples – Italic, Etruscan, Greek – and the sanctuary of Punta Campanella constitutes the focal point.

It was in this phase that the territory of Surrentum was organised. In the Trinità district in the Municipality of Piano di Sorrento, the first excavations, conducted between 1987 and 1990 on the occasion of the construction of a school, led to the discovery of an important settlement of the Chalcolithic Gaudo facies, along with attestations of the Archaic period.[20] The Gaudo facies necropolis is dated to the second half of the 3rd century BC. Five small chamber tombs, excavated in the grey local tuff, each with an access vestibule, were discovered. In contrast, a building in blocks of tuff oriented north-east/south-west and some pits are dated to the mid-6th century BC (Figures 3.3–3.4).

The building was damaged by a flood in the 4th century BC, after which it was rebuilt with reused materials and a different orientation. Divided into five rooms facing an open space, it is hypothesised that it served a religious function, given the presence of architectural material from the roof, including antefixes, votive coroplastic figurines and numerous fragments of black-glaze ware, as well as its proximity to the spring of San Massimo. In the late 3rd or early 2nd century BC, the area underwent further reorganisation, with the creation of an industrial area consisting of furnaces for making roof tiles and processing glass. This phase, too, saw frequent floods, with material washed downhill and the consequent end of production. However, the settlement continued to be occupied until the eruption of 79 AD, which deposited a layer of lapilli about 60 cm thick, sealing the area.

In the late 1990s and the first few years of this century, in an area slightly further uphill (Figure 3.5) – and thus even closer to the spring of San Massimo – a large cluster of burials was discovered.[21]

Consisting of 66 tombs, it was organised into lots that probably corresponded to different families. They were mainly in cavities lined and covered with slabs of tuff or earth-pit graves, oriented east-west, in some cases surrounded by a wall composed of small blocks of local grey tuff; the most common approach was inhumation, although cases of primary and secondary incineration are also documented. The most ancient grave goods are

22 *The Sorrentine Peninsula based on archaeological sources*

Figure 3.3 Piano di Sorrento, Via San Massimo. Building found in Trinità district. 1987–1990 excavations.

Credit: Claude Albore Livadie.

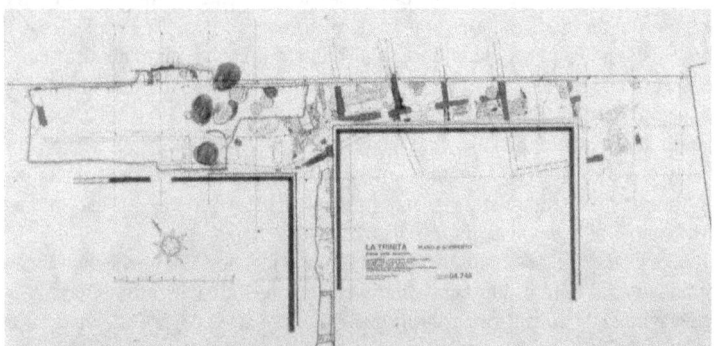

Figure 3.4 Piano di Sorrento, Via San Massimo. Floor plan of the building found in Trinità district. 1987–1990 excavations.

Credit: Claude Albore Livadie.

The Sorrentine Peninsula based on archaeological sources 23

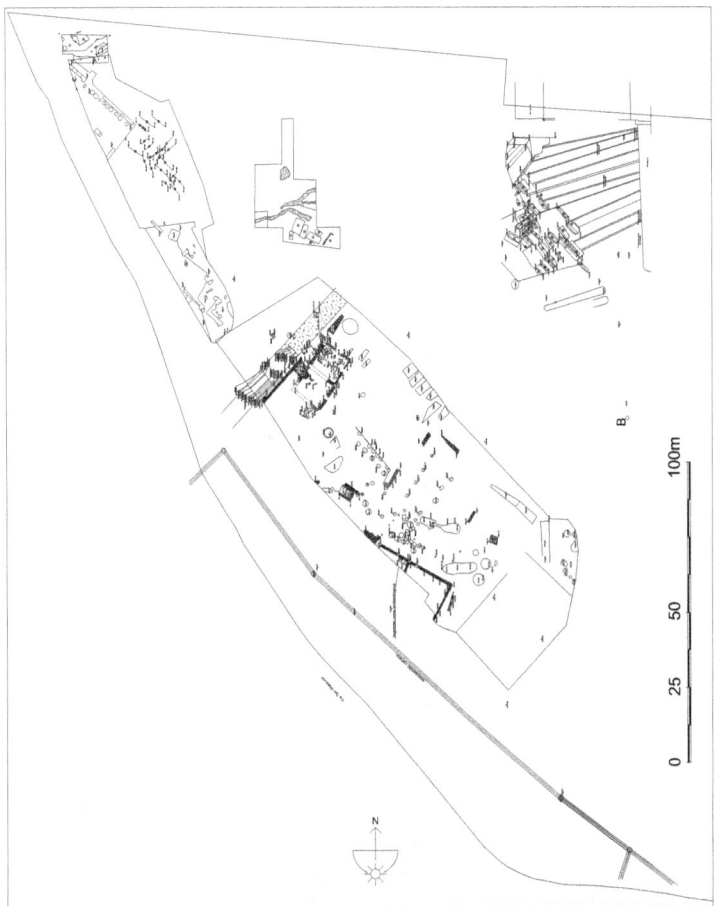

Figure 3.5 Piano di Sorrento, Via San Massimo. Site plan of 1999–2004 excavations.
Credit: Soprintendenza Archive.

characterised by the association of *bucchero*, Attic black-figure vessels and black-glaze ware, as well as common achromatic ceramics and personalised grave goods consisting of bronze fibulae and silver rings. In the vicinity was a small building composed of a single chamber and an access room, around which were found pits filled with dumped materials. The adjacent tombs are also dated to the period from the 6th to the 4th centuries BC (Figure 3.6).

In the late Republican period, an aqueduct and furnaces were built. The entire area was destroyed and definitively abandoned in 79 AD.

24 *The Sorrentine Peninsula based on archaeological sources*

Figure 3.6 Piano di Sorrento, Via San Massimo. Detail of the archaic building.
Credit: Soprintendenza Archive.

The recent discovery in Via Mortora San Liborio, in the Municipality of Piano di Sorrento, of a paved road (Figure 3.7), clearly from the Roman epoch but not precisely datable, confirms the centrality of the site in the district of Trinità: the road is oriented south-east/north-west and thus ran between the upland of Trinità and Sorrento.[22]

Indeed, the reading of the city in the Roman period, especially from the 1st century BC onwards, is much clearer. Within the short circuit of walls, public buildings such as the theatre and the baths were constructed and the forum was established. An additional feature characteristic of the territory was the appearance of grand private residences,[23] for example, the villa situated near Piazza della Vittoria and the San Paolo convent, traditionally associated with the exile of Agrippa Postumus, who had been heir to the Roman Emperor Augustus, later falling into disgrace, the villa near Palazzo Caporiva in the grounds of the Hotel Vittoria[24] and the large seaside villa in the Bagni della Regina Giovanna district near Capo di Sorrento.[25] The emperor himself seems to have played a role here since the presence of a place of exile for a prince indicates that there was an imperial property in the city.

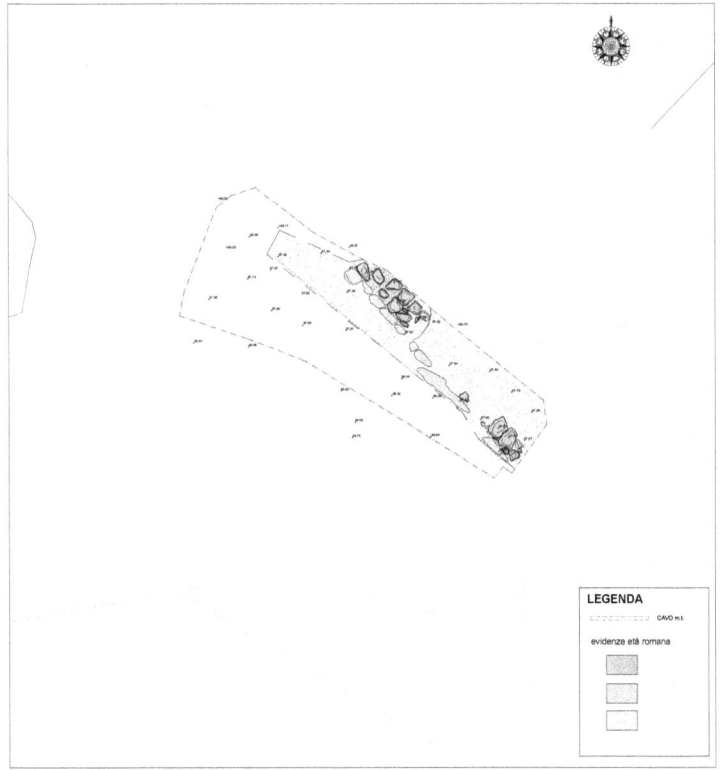

Figure 3.7 Piano di Sorrento, Via Mortora San Liborio. Roman road.
Credit: Soprintendenza Archive.

All these factors significantly affected the development of the territory. The sources refer to the area's famous wine production, for which there was a flourishing market that involved the presence of workshops making transport amphorae. These have been identified in Villa Fiorentino, where many ceramic discards were discovered, indicating a centre of production.[26]

Notes

1 It seems appropriate here to recall the extensive toponymic study, with topographical insights as well, on Surrentum, by Poccetti 2016.
2 On this topic a useful overview is offered by Bonghi Jovino 2008. See also Osanna, Rescigno 2021, especially for its Archaic period of occupation's development of the

Sarno Valley and the Sorrentine Peninsula. In particular, pages 214–222 emphasise well the geographical aspect of the peninsula.
3 For a summary on literary sources, see Guzzo 2016, 61–67. More in detail Mele 2014.
4 Federico 1998.
5 Strab, V, 4, 8.
6 St. Byz, s.v. Συρρέντον.
7 On this topic see Rescigno, Senatore 2009, 415–462.
8 The data come mainly from necropolis: Albore Livadie 2001; Sorrentino, Viscione 2001.
9 Savarese 1963; Budetta 2001, 15–22; Bonghi Jovino 2008, 94–95.
10 On the oldest excavations of the necropolis, see Bonghi Jovino 1982. On the most recent investigations, there is only Budetta 2001.
11 News in Sampaolo 1984, 505–506, 1990, 109–118, 1992a, 133–140, 1992b, 99–109; Budetta 1996, 35–138.
12 Zancani Montuoro 1983, 1987.
13 On the topic, much discussed in the literature, see Breglia Pulci Doria 1996 and recently Mele 2016.
14 Russo 1997, 53–57; Laudonia 2013.
15 Mingazzini, Pfister 1946, 219–225.
16 Rescigno 2010.
17 Rescigno 2010.
18 On these topics, see Osanna, Rescigno 2021, with bibliography.
19 Poccetti 2010.
20 Albore Livadie 1990, 1992, 2010; Russo 1998, 44–45; Budetta 1999, 19–20.
21 On this necropolis, the only publication is Rispoli 2013.
22 On the Via Minervia in this section, see Russo 1998.
23 On this subject, we refer especially to Russo 1999.
24 On this villa, see recently Di Franco, Laudonia 2022, with bibliography.
25 Filser et al. 2017.
26 Breglia Pulci Doria 1996, 182.

4 Access to the sanctuary
The Via Minervia

At this stage, it is appropriate to indicate what structures and signs of human activities linked to antiquity are currently visible in the area of Punta Campanella, specifically on the promontory at the tip of the Sorrentine Peninsula bound by the inlets known as Baia di Ieranto to the south-east and Cala di Mitigliano to the north-west. The Via Minervia originally started in the city of Stabiae and passed through Surrentum before reaching the cape.[1] In the stretch from Cancello, the highest known point of the ancient road, it ran along the steep hillside, requiring substruction works[2] of varying magnitude in many places. These include imposing walls in *opus incertum*, some bound with mortar (Figure 4.1) and some without, using roughly hewn interlocking blocks (Figure 4.2).

In other cases, there are only dry-stone retaining walls (Figures 4.3–4.4).

Figure 4.1 Massa Lubrense. Opus incertum section of the Via Minervia.
Credit: Soprintendenza Archive.

DOI: 10.4324/9781032647548-4

28 *Access to the sanctuary*

Figure 4.2 Massa Lubrense. Polygonal masonry section of the Via Minervia.
Credit: Soprintendenza Archive.

Figure 4.3 Massa Lubrense, Via Minervia. Assay 13. Terracing of the road.
Credit: Soprintendenza Archive.

Access to the sanctuary 29

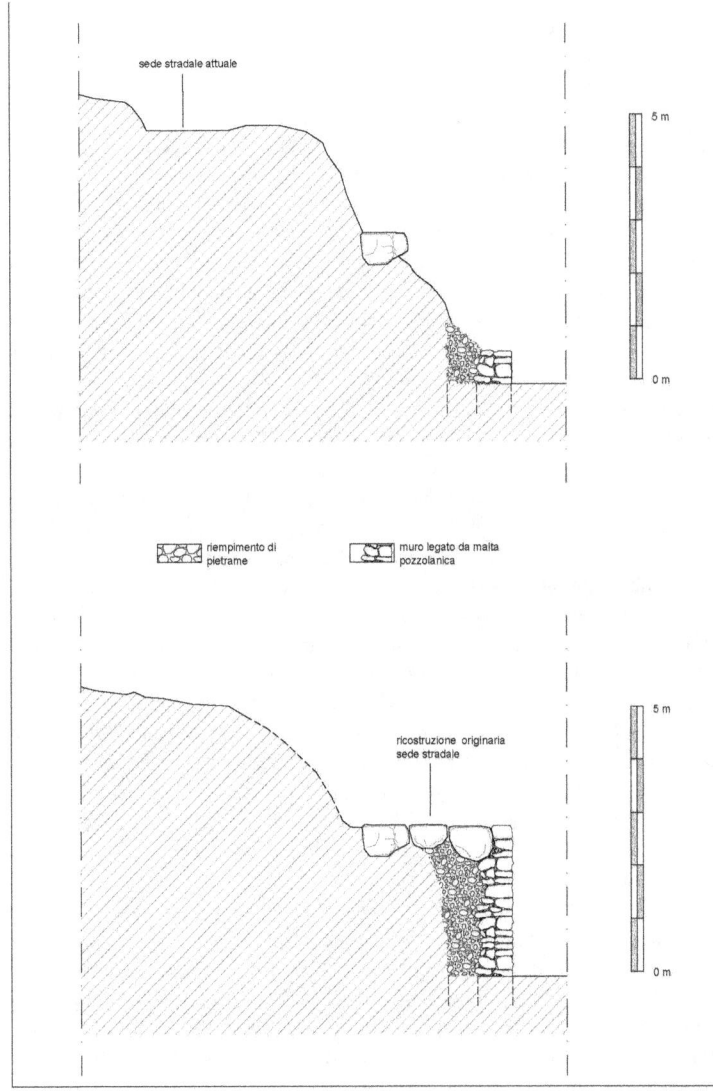

Figure 4.4 Massa Lubrense, Via Minervia. Drawings of the current state of the road and reconstruction.

Credit: Soprintendenza Archive.

The road itself was composed of large sub-circular flagstones in local limestone and was bounded by kerbs which on the uphill side were partly carved into the rock.[3]

In the Fossa di Papa district, large stretches of beaten earth have been found beneath the modern paving (Assay 8) and the medieval flagstones (Assay 10). These correspond to a road that, in the best-conserved stretches, is 1.6 m wide and, in places, is delimited on the downhill side by dry-stone walls. Unfortunately, the total absence in all the assays of ceramic material meant that it was not possible to draw up an accurate chronology for the finds. It can, however, be deduced that this road predated the medieval paved road and was in continuous use over a long period. Indeed, Assay 8 revealed a vertical succession of beaten earth layers that underwent maintenance and repair. The excavation shows that an initial footpath, narrow and uneven across the rocks, was at some point replaced by a proper road, also in beaten earth but wider and better structured, as cuttings in the outcropping rock made by the road builders seem to confirm. These cuts, dated to the road's most ancient phase, were subsequently used for laying the flagstones of the medieval paved road.

From the available data, it may be supposed that the modern road between the Cancello and Fossa di Papa districts roughly retraces the ancient road, with a few variations and adaptations in response to mainly natural phenomena. Indeed, although Assays 3 and 4 yielded no new elements regarding the most ancient route, they did show that even in recent times, the road has shifted horizontally due to landslides along the ridge, while Assays 5, 6 and 9 highlighted collapses, with relative repairs and modifications, of the rock-face of the most ancient cuttings.

Assay 7, corresponding to a retaining wall in *opus incertum*, yielded no trace of the top of the Roman-era wall, which had clearly collapsed, requiring the course of the road to be shifted uphill.

An interesting stratigraphic element that has emerged from some assays (3, 6, and 7) is the presence of traces, of varying abundance, of grey volcanic ash linked to eruptions of Vesuvius in recent times, some of which were no longer in primary contexts. The investigations of the stretch of road running from the Cancello to the Fossa di Papa districts found no limestone paving of any kind nor traces that might indicate its presence. The only possible exception is Assay 1, which found a stretch of carriageway in beaten earth bordered by cuttings in the rock and signs of maintenance and repairs over a long period. In addition, the landslides occurring over time were tackled by shifting the course of the road further up the slope.

The investigations conducted in 2015 and 2016 made it possible to identify the ancient paved road in various places, but only between Fossa di Papa and Punta Campanella. Specifically, Assays 11 (Figure 4.5), 13 (Figure 4.6) and 14 (Figures 4.7–4.8) revealed stretches in a good state of conservation, which may be added to the segment still *in situ* and usable as far as Punta Campanella.

Access to the sanctuary 31

Figure 4.5 Massa Lubrense, Via Minervia. Assay 11. Ancient road section.
Credit: Soprintendenza Archive.

Figure 4.6 Massa Lubrense, Via Minervia. Assay 13. Ancient road section.
Credit: Soprintendenza Archive.

32 Access to the sanctuary

Figure 4.7 Massa Lubrense, Via Minervia. Assay 14. Ancient road section.
Credit: Soprintendenza Archive.

Figure 4.8 Massa Lubrense, Via Minervia. Assay 14. Ancient road section.
Credit: Soprintendenza Archive.

Access to the sanctuary 33

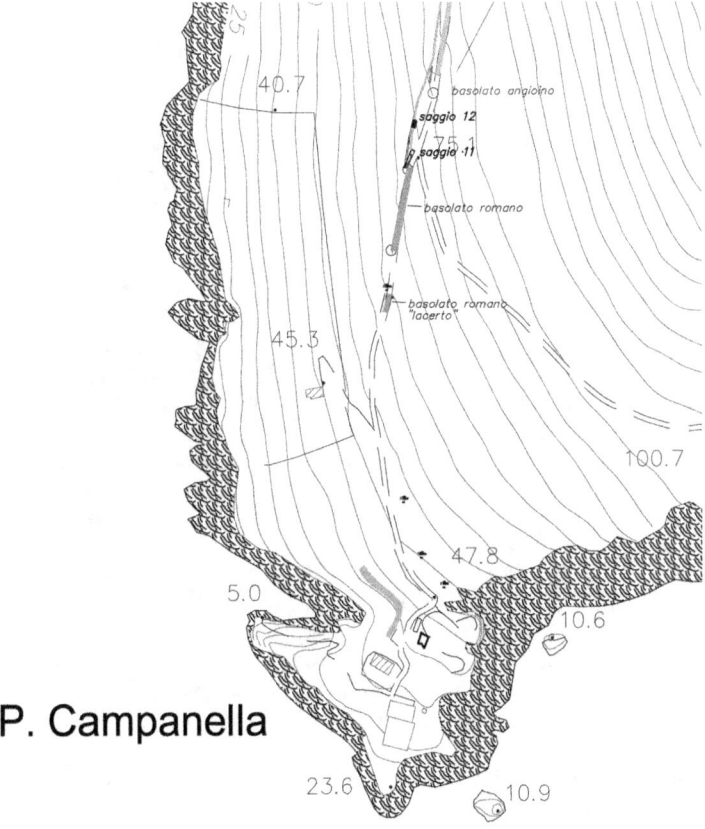

Figure 4.9 Massa Lubrense, Via Minervia. Site plan of the last route.
Credit: Soprintendenza Archive.

The assays have shown that near the promontory, the ancient road was lower than it is currently (Figure 4.9).

Indeed, in its final stretch, where it runs along the west side of the promontory, the Via Minervia departs from the modern road, bending sharply westwards and dropping towards the shore, subsequently reaching the lower terrace near Punta Campanella further south. The 2015 investigations identified segments of the last 270 m but, unfortunately, also recorded its partial disappearance in some places due to collapses and landslides.

In the stretch further north (Assay 8), the paved road had no doubt been preceded by simple beaten earth. Indeed, Assay 8 documented a stratigraphic succession of routes that criss-crossed each other among the rocks (Figure 4.10),[4] bringing to light along its western edge a horizontal succession

Figure 4.10 Massa Lubrense, Via Minervia. Assay 8. Beaten earth layers.
Credit: Soprintendenza Archive.

of highly compact levels of beaten earth consisting of pyroclastic material with limestone fragments.

There are at least two layers of roadway: the natural limestone bedrock was roughly levelled, filling in the gaps to create an even flat surface, on top of which levels of beaten earth were laid, in which traces of use are still conserved.

Notes

1 The path of the road and its evidence are in Russo 1998; Caputo 2004.
2 On the substructions see Caputo 2004, 81–83; Budetta, Cannavacciuolo, Rizzo 2018.
3 The totality of these data is derived from excavations along the Via Minervia in 2015 and 2016, published partially in Budetta, Cannavacciuolo, Rizzo 2018.
4 Budetta, Cannavacciuolo, Rizzo 2018, 366–367.

5 Punta Campanella
The archaeological record

Near the cape, the Via Minervia passes a small tank (Figures 5.1–5.2), originally positioned on the uphill side of the ancient road.

Represented in a drawing by Mingazzini as a circular structure and interpreted by him as a *specula*,[1] it consists of a square base (2.7 x 2.7 m), on which rests the semicircular basin (max. width 1.16 m), whose inner surface is covered by a thick layer of hydraulic cement. The curvature of the semicircle is oriented south/south-east, while the straight wall appears to have been partially built against the hillside. As in almost all other cases in this location, the masonry is composed of pieces of limestone of varying dimensions, bound by a weak earth-based mortar.

Figure 5.1 Punta Campanella. Entrance to the sanctuary. Semicircular basin. View from above.

Credit: Author.

DOI: 10.4324/9781032647548-5

Figure 5.2 Punta Campanella. Entrance to the sanctuary. Semicircular basin. Side view.
Credit: Author.

Figure 5.3 Punta Campanella. Entrance to the sanctuary. Terminal section of the Via Minervia. View from the north.
Credit: Author.

Judging from what is still visible today, the road led directly to the first (i.e., the lowest) terrace of Punta Campanella. In the excavations of 1987, the large volumes of earth that covered the final stretch of the Via Minervia were removed, revealing a paved road (2.17 m wide), including a stretch 10.7 m long which was cut from the rock (Figures 5.3–5.4).[2]

Figure 5.4 Punta Campanella. Entrance to the sanctuary. Terminal section of the Via Minervia. View from the south.

Credit: Author.

Along the western edge, the road shows clear signs of repairs in Roman concrete, made with chips of tuff and brick, no doubt attributable to a late operation to raise the road. The holes chipped in the clearly worn flagstones, intended to improve the adherence of the new layer of concrete, can also be read in this light. Running along the entire east side was a large cistern in limestone *opus incertum* (4.47 m wide), today partly collapsed, divided into two vaulted chambers (max. width 1.60 and 1.50 m) (Figure 5.5).[3]

Also, on the east side of the road, unlike the west side, the kerb was absent. Instead, there was a low wall cut from the rock, partly covered in a layer of *opus signinum* (Figure 5.6), which ran along the edge of the cistern, with the road sloping gradually downhill.

At the highest point of the cistern, at the north end, there was a small basin, probably for drainage, given the presence of a small channel oriented east-west leading towards it. The channel is believed to have drained waters from the second terrace, which was on the same level as the top of the cistern.

On the western side of the road were other structures, some of which were visible to Mingazzini, who called them "exedrae". Partly investigated in 1987

38 *Punta Campanella*

Figure 5.5 Punta Campanella. Entrance to the sanctuary. Historical photo of the cistern on the side of the Via Minervia.

Credit: Archeoclub Massa Lubrense.

Figure 5.6 Punta Campanella. Entrance to the sanctuary. Terminal section of the Via Minervia.

Credit: Author.

Figure 5.7 Punta Campanella. Entrance to the sanctuary. Structures west of the Via Minervia.

Credit: Author.

(Figures 5.7–5.8), they lie within a sturdy retaining wall on the west side, visible from the sea (Figure 5.9).[4]

The first, rectangular and partially dug out of the ground, was used to collect rainwater draining from the road. On its south side is a long retaining wall running perpendicular to the road (i.e., oriented east-west). On the south side of this wall, on a slightly lower level, there are two adjacent rectangular structures (4.94 x 2.28 m),[5] next to which, on an even lower level towards the west, there are the remains of a semicircular structure in *opus incertum* (max. width 3.24 m).[6] All these structures are slightly out of alignment with the road. The two adjacent rectangular structures are each marked by an internal wall built against the wall that divides them. They are lined with hydraulic mortar and paved with *opus signinum*. A third rectangular structure aligned with these two was seen and drawn by Mingazzini and Pfister.[7]

The building technique for all these structures was the same, with small differences. In some parts of the masonry, such as the inclusion of fragments of brick, probably reused, in addition to the limestone, possibly of more recent

40 Punta Campanella

Figure 5.8 Punta Campanella. Entrance to the sanctuary. 3D model from the west and from the sea.

Credit: Soprintendenza Archive.

Figure 5.9 Punta Campanella. Entrance to the sanctuary. 3D model from the west.

Credit: Soprintendenza Archive.

execution. The very small size of these structures, their position near the cliff edge, their partial excavation in the ground and, lastly, the walls lined with *opus signinum* all suggest a function linked to rainwater drainage, or at least that they were originally exposed to the elements. There is no doubt, however, that the first of the rectangular structures, which has partially collapsed since 1987 (see Figure 2.4), was a cistern, as the presence of a hole at the bottom of the west wall demonstrates.[8]

On the same level but on the eastern side, there was a broad space whose character was revealed by the excavations of 1987.[9] Here, there is a portico

Figure 5.10 Punta Campanella. First terrace. View from above.
Credit: Soprintendenza Archive.

marked by a line of pillars (0.50 x 0.50 m, separated from each other by a distance of 2.3 m), of which only the rectangular bases, evenly spaced, remain on the ground (Figure 5.10).

The paving consisted of a base layer of mortar, on which there was a layer of *opus signinum*, probably completed with some other material. The two ends of the portico (max. length 14 m, max. width 2 m) were plausibly closed with semicircular walls, of which only the eastern one is conserved. On the north side of the portico, a short corridor oriented north-south led to a threshold (1.26 x 0.70 m) with holes drilled for seating double doors. The threshold gave access to a symmetrical double flight of steps, one to the left and one to the right, carved in the rock steps (1.34 x 0.35 m) leading up to the second terrace. The rock face on the north side of the steps was lined with limestone *opus incertum* (Figures 5.11–5.14).

The second and third terraces to the north were investigated in 2004 by means of two assays. The second terrace, still partly covered in earth and vegetation, has cuttings in the rock to make the area flatter. The construction of one of the two gun batteries in the reign of Murat entailed the demolition of any archaeological structures that may have been conserved, but a sort of rectangular exedra seems to have been carved into the rock face at the eastern end (length 10 m). Carved into its back wall are a number of unaligned shelves, above which are clear traces of at least eight quadrangular recesses of varying dimensions (Figures 5.15–5.16).[10]

Figure 5.11 Punta Campanella. First terrace. View from north of the terrace and the flight of steps carved in the rock.

Credit: Author.

Figure 5.12 Punta Campanella. First terrace. View from the south-west of the terrace and the flight of steps carved in the rock.

Credit: Author.

Punta Campanella 43

Figure 5.13 Punta Campanella. First terrace. View from the west of the flight of steps carved in the rock.

Credit: Author.

Figure 5.14 Punta Campanella. First terrace. View from the south of the flight of steps carved in the rock.

Credit: Author.

Figure 5.15 Punta Campanella. Second terrace. Worked rock wall.
Credit: Author.

Almost parallel to the exedra but about 2 m further forward is a limestone threshold (1.87 x 0.55 m) with holes for seating a set of double doors flanked by two squared blocks of tuff (Figure 5.17).

The assay of 2004 brought to light a small area of this terrace paved with a layer of concrete and a row of squared limestone blocks (length 6.59 m). Where these blocks are missing, blocks of tuff, perhaps belonging to the foundations or even to a previous phase of the structure, oriented east-west, can be seen. On the limestone blocks, circular grooves for seating columns (diam. 0.49 m) are conserved (Figures 5.18–5.20).

The third terrace, the highest in this sector, is separated from the upland to the north by a deep cleft in the rock, in which there are ancient steps leading down to the so-called *approdo di levante* (Eastern Landing) (Figure 5.21).

According to Mingazzini,[11] the steps, mostly carved in the rock, were partly built over a retaining wall in *opus reticulatum* (Figures 5.22–5.23).

The walls on the north side of the third terrace that served to protect the gun batteries built in the reign of Murat effectively blocked access to these steps. Visible on the west side of the circular battery, there are two perpendicular walls of uncertain date (2.22 and 3.83 m long), whose orientation matches that of the terrace. On their west side is a quadrangular block of masonry (Figures 5.24–5.25).

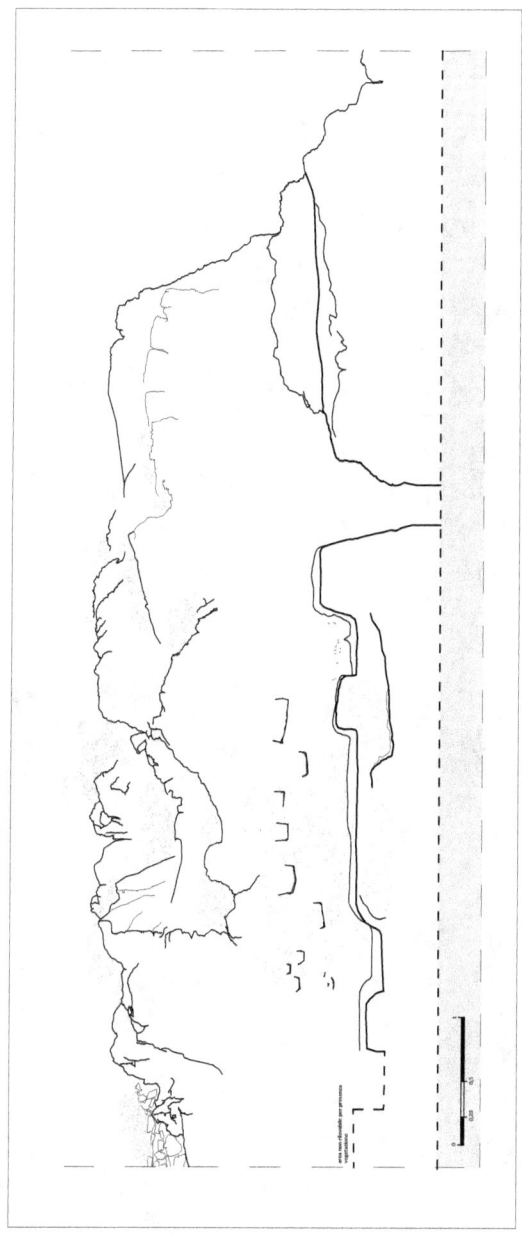

Figure 5.16 Punta Campanella. Second terrace. Perspective drawing of worked rock wall.
Credit: Author.

46 Punta Campanella

Figure 5.17 Punta Campanella. Second terrace. Threshold and pillars.
Credit: Soprintendenza Archive.

Figure 5.18 Punta Campanella. Second terrace. Foundation of colonnaded portico.
Credit: Soprintendenza Archive.

Punta Campanella 47

Figure 5.19 Punta Campanella. Second terrace. Foundation of colonnaded portico. Detail of the circular grooves for seating columns.

Credit: Soprintendenza Archive.

Figure 5.20 Punta Campanella. Second terrace. Foundation of colonnaded portico. Detail of the circular grooves for seating columns.

Credit: Soprintendenza Archive.

Figure 5.21 Punta Campanella. Third terrace. Murattian wall closing the east flight of steps carved in the rock.

Credit: Author.

Punta Campanella 49

Figure 5.22 Punta Campanella. Between the third and fourth terraces. East flight of steps carved in the rock.

Credit: Author.

Figure 5.23 Punta Campanella. Between the third and fourth terraces. East flight of steps carved in the rock.

Credit: Author.

Figure 5.24 Punta Campanella. Third terrace. Walls and structures.
Credit: Author.

Figure 5.25 Punta Campanella. Third terrace. Walls and structures.
Credit: Author.

The final terrace, the fourth, is situated beyond the cleft, with the steps leading down to the Eastern Landing. Here, a long wall in *opus incertum* is conserved, built directly against the straightened rock face in order to create a back wall oriented east-west for a series of spaces separated from each other by perpendicular walls in a "comb" pattern. A little to the east, further down the slope, are the remains of a large cistern largely carved out of the rock and covered in *opus signinum* (9.73 x 4.32 m).[12]

Uphill to the north-east, where the terrain does not form a proper terrace, there is another rectangular structure entirely carved from the rock.

Notes

1. Mingazzini, Pfister 1946, 146, fig. 34, structure no. n.
2. Mingazzini, Pfister 1946 did not see this section of the road; they sensed, however, the path further north in an east-west orientation, so see Mingazzini, Pfister 1946, 145, fig. 34, structure no. i.
3. It currently remains in doubt what Mingazzini and Pfister saw of this area. We could speculate that Mingazzini, Pfister 1946, 145, fig. 34, structures no. g^1-g^2, could be part of the cistern walls, as the description mentions vaulted chambers. It seems rather strange that Mingazzini did not see the large cistern, which is practically always above ground. The authors also quote a *opus signinum* floor, which presumably refers to the walkable top of the cistern. The steps, on the other hand, marked with no. h, is no longer visible. Although the planimetry is not entirely accurate, these structures are aligned with the so-called "exedras" and thus distort the reading of the context by no small margin.
4. Mingazzini, Pfister 1946, 145, fig. 34, structures nos. e^1-e^2. Interpreted as terrace walls.
5. Mingazzini, Pfister 1946, 145, fig. 34, structures nos. c^1-c^2. Interpreted as exedras. The authors claim that the doubling of the wall is actually a seat. The purpose, for all these exedras, was to sit and admire the sea in the authors' opinion.
6. Mingazzini, Pfister 1946, 145, fig. 34, structure no. b. Interpreted as exedras, with a merely decorative function.
7. Mingazzini, Pfister 1946, 145, fig. 34, structure no. c^3. Interpreted always as exedras.
8. Of this structure, Mingazzini, Pfister 1946, 145, fig. 34, saw only a few walls. Furthermore, behind the rectangular rooms known as "exedras", Mingazzini, Pfister 1946, 145, fig. 34, structure no. f, pointed out unalloyed square blocks, which, in their opinion, can be traced back to an Archaic period connected to the temple of Athena.
9. Mingazzini, Pfister 1946, 146, fig. 34, structures nos. g^3-g^4, saw the *opus signinum* floor and a curved structure, which they do not describe.
10. This could be Mingazzini, Pfister 1946, 145, fig. 34, structure no. k. The authors speak of a cistern covered with *opus signinum*, which, however, does not exist on the lower terrace. The westernmost part of the wall is currently barely visible due to vegetation, but a north-south facing wall corner is present.
11. Mingazzini, Pfister 1946, 146, fig. 34.
12. Mingazzini, Pfister 1946, 146, fig. 34, structures nos. m, p.

6 Analysis of the context
The sanctuary of Athena

What emerges from the existing structures in the area of the promontory is the substantial homogeneity of architectural techniques, despite being unequivocally attributable to more than one phase, and the organic structure of the site as a whole (Figures 6.1–6.2).

As Werner Johannowsky insightfully points out,[1] neither the excavations conducted in the past nor the current analysis of the site have found any structures with a residential function, as also noted by Beloch and Mingazzini. The existence of an imperial villa, or rather a military post, linked to Tiberius' stay on the island of Capri is purely circumstantial and relies on the passage in Suetonius that tells of the emperor's disquiet and the need to have naval vessels always ready for whatever circumstance.[2] The lack of large structures and the discovery in 1987 of the apparently 'public' paved road leading directly to the tip of the peninsula all tend to undermine the hypothesis that the masonry structures visible today belong to a residence.[3]

Today, the site can be divided into three sectors: the road, the terraces and the structures beyond the cleft on the north side of the third terrace.

The first sector, unfortunately partly destroyed by post-ancient structures, coincides with the terminal stretch of the Via Minervia and is characterised by sturdy retaining walls. It contains infrastructure mainly for channelling rainwater (Figure 6.3), although the semicircular structure west of the road and the two adjacent rectangular structures may have had some other function.

For example, faced seawards, they may have been related to preparation for access to the sanctuary. It is unknown whether there were other structures where the medieval tower stands today or, indeed, where the lighthouse operator's house once stood, although it is perfectly possible that other structures are near the medieval tower.

From this level on the western side, there is a long flight of steps carved in the rock. Oriented east-west, the steps lead down to the so-called *approdo di ponente* ("Western Landing"), a small natural harbour sheltered by a small inlet, ideal for arriving by sea. In any case, whether arriving by land or sea, from this access point, the sacred area stretched upwards, the porticoes marking and imposing order on the natural terraces. At the foot of the slope was a

DOI: 10.4324/9781032647548-6

Analysis of the context 53

Figure 6.1 Site plan of Punta Campanella showing all ancient structures.
Credit: Author.

crypto-portico, perhaps with a colonnade on the south side,[4] the roof of which served to extend the terrace above, accessed via twin flights of steps. The conserved bases arranged along an east-west axis may have marked the façade of the structure, or they may have corresponded to a central row of pillars dividing it into two parts.

The double flight of steps carved in the rock and apparently obscured by the portico in front of it led up to another more even terrace (Figure 6.4).

The ground level of this terrace coincided on the western side with the upper level of the large cistern with two vaulted chambers, the roof of which is believed to have extended the terrace towards the road on the western side, thereby functioning as both a cistern and a substruction. On the eastern side,

54 *Analysis of the context*

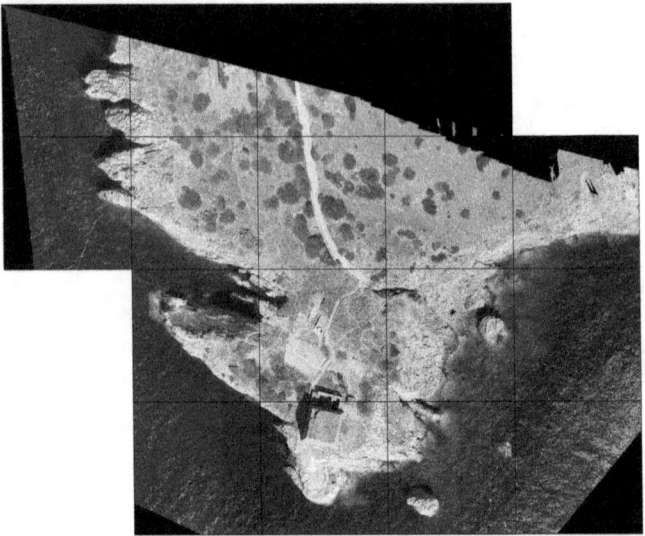

Figure 6.2 Orthophoto of Punta Campanella.
Credit: Soprintendenza Archive.

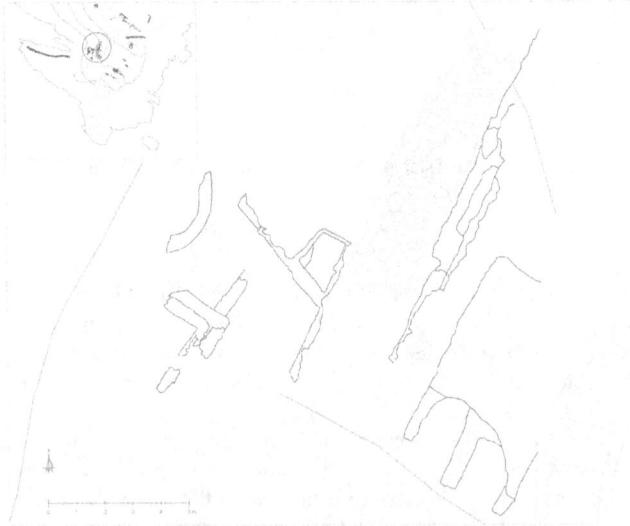

Figure 6.3 Punta Campanella. Floor plan of the entrance to the sanctuary.
Credit: Author.

Analysis of the context 55

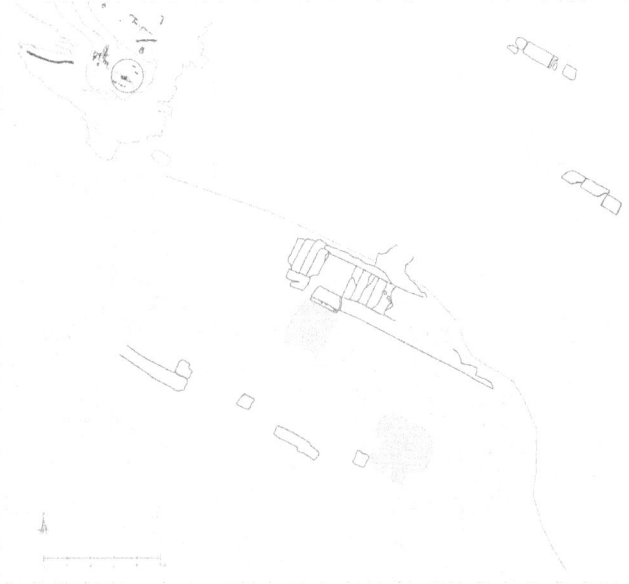

Figure 6.4 Punta Campanella. Floor plan of the first and second terraces.
Credit: Author.

the remains of a small structure carved in the rock extend to the edge of the cliff. On its back wall were unaligned shelves, probably for placing votive offerings, and recesses for slabs, also of a devotional nature, bearing either inscriptions or reliefs. Discovered on this level was a row of limestone blocks oriented east-west, in which the east corner and the circular traces of the seating for the columns, probably part of the portico that covered this terrace on the north side, can be seen. The technique used, i.e., rectangular blocks with recesses in which to seat columns otherwise without bases, is attested in the Triangular Forum in Pompeii, whose portico is dated to the 2nd century BC.[5] In any case, the presence of a threshold on the lower level with double doors giving access to the double flight of steps suggests that this sector was of vital importance and, when necessary, was closed to the public.

The third and final terrace, where one of Murat's gun batteries was installed, was accessible via another flight of steps oriented north-south, access to which was across a threshold. Unlike the previous terrace, this one is not flat or levelled. It mostly consists of a steep outcrop looking onto the so-called Eastern Landing. Almost nothing remains of this sector due to the destruction that took place at the start of the 19th century. The 2004 excavation led to the discovery of two perpendicular walls (the north end of the

56 *Analysis of the context*

north-south wall joins another with an east-west orientation) that closed off a structure at its eastern end. Inside the structure, there was another wall, again composed of limestone chips, probably linked to the Murat period. To the west, a quadrangular block, not yet fully excavated, is of doubtful interpretation. In any case, the function of these structures was to stabilise the edge of the terrace, not coincidentally used by the French for a gun battery, given its advantageous position. If we suppose that on the terrace below, the limestone blocks belonged to the colonnade of the portico, it may be assumed that the cult building was on this higher level.

The eastern flight of steps, which makes use of a natural cleft in the rock, oriented east-west, is of key importance. Today, however, its western end is not visible since it is obscured by a wall made of limestone chips built by the French with the clear aim of preventing access to the gun batteries from the sea (see Figure 5.21). The steps are believed to have led directly from the water to the second or third terrace, i.e., to the heart of the ancient sanctuary, thereafter following a route below the modern road before bending southwards. This deduction is supported by the inscription on the rock face near the bottom of the steps (Figure 6.5), a dedication by two *meddices*, priests of the goddess Minerva, who are believed to have built (or restored) the eastern steps or, according to a recent less plausible opinion, a lighthouse.[6]

Figure 6.5 Punta Campanella. Oscan inscription on the north side wall of the flight of steps carved in the rock.

Credit: Author.

Analysis of the context 57

On closer inspection, the steps (Figure 6.6), once seen as meeting the need to reach a second landing stage, should rather be read in relation to the presence of a small karst cave situated on the north side of the cleft at the foot of the high limestone cliff (Figure 6.7).

Figure 6.6 Punta Campanella. 3D model from east.
Credit: Soprintendenza Archive.

Figure 6.7 Punta Campanella. Picture of the cave and the end of the east flight of steps carved in the rock.
Credit: Author.

58 Analysis of the context

Indeed, in contrast to the situation on the other (western) side of the promontory, the rocks on this side make the presence of a proper landing highly improbable. In addition, the last few steps turn towards the flat space in front of the cave as if leading to its entrance (Figure 6.8).

Inside the cave, there are the remains of masonry structures on the west side. The meaning of this cave is a topic to which we shall return.

The final sector, in contrast, is made up of the spaces arranged in a 'comb' pattern along the slope beyond the cleft, with which the small semicircular basin to the east of them may also be associated. Their function remains uncertain, although the presence inside the sanctuary of structures linked to its operation, such as accommodation or rooms for the consumption of food, cannot be excluded.

Regarding the phases of the site as a whole, it is possible at the moment to identify only two building episodes: the first is characterised by masonry composed of limestone chips, generically classifiable as *opus incertum*, irregular and bound by a weak mortar. In the western sector, near the road, successive restorations and repairs using limestone chips mixed with reused materials are visible.

Within what is believed to be the sacred area, despite the lack of elements that would enable reliable dating, hypotheses can be made on the basis of the

Figure 6.8 Punta Campanella. Photo of the end of the east flight of steps carved in the rock as seen from the cave.

Credit: Archeoclub Massa Lubrense.

architectural features. The structure of the portico on the first terrace, with one or two short sides in the form of an apse, has a precise parallel in the villa of the *ambulatio* in Baia, dated roughly to the late Republican period, but within the 2nd century BC.[7] The parallel with Baia and coeval sanctuaries in the Latium region[8] is even stronger if the pillar bases correspond to the central spine of a double corridor.

In the same way, the roadbed of the *Via Minervia* in the stretch between Cancello and Punta Campanella is characterised by the near absence of concrete, there being a preference for earthworks bolstered on the seaward side by stones without mortar. A substruction in the form of a buttress, entirely in *opus incertum*, is conserved in only one point. Disregarding the repairs and restorations, this stretch of road may be dated to the mid-2nd century BC or perhaps a little later. Although it proves little, the use in the substructions of *opus incertum* bedded with mortar, together with a polygonal dry-stone structure made of interlocking blocks, supports a late-Republican chronology[9] and dating to the 2nd or early 1st century BC would be entirely plausible.[10] Lastly, the inscription provides a valid chronological marker, framing a period from the beginning of the 3rd to the late 2nd century BC,[11] but more plausibly the latter.

If we seek, therefore, to assemble the pieces of this puzzle, we must start by affirming that at least the paved road, the crypto-portico on the first terrace and the portico on the second terrace are all from the same phase, and so perhaps is the dedication of the Oscan inscription of the Eastern Landing. Indeed, from a strictly architectural point of view, the arrangement of the structures indicates that they were all part of the same design: given the particular conformation of the terrain, not conducive to transport, the paved road, partly carved in the rock, cannot have been conceived or built in a later phase than the structures on the terraces. In addition, the road, like the cistern that is structurally attached to it, is perfectly perpendicular with respect to the portico on the second terrace and thus with the natural terracing, which was artificially accentuated in many places, but also to the double flight of steps leading up from the first terrace, the row of blocks of the portico on the second terrace and the threshold granting access to the third terrace (Figure 6.9).

The road and the portico are thus the fruit of a single architectural project adapted to the natural conformation of the terrain. In fact, the few structures that have emerged on the third terrace, as well as the surviving walls on the terrace beyond the cleft, are aligned with each other, although their orientation differs slightly with respect to the first two terraces. Thus, in this phase, the sanctuary may have been refurbished, partly in a monumental style, with each space assuming a specific function within a pre-existing but less complex cult area.

Access to the cult building, believed to have been on the second or third terrace and hence reached via the double flight of steps, was initially via a covered portico facing the sea. In addition to the crypto-portico currently visible on the first terrace, there may have been another such structure where the

60 *Analysis of the context*

Figure 6.9 Site plan of Punta Campanella showing all ancient structures and their orientation.

Credit: Author.

medieval tower stands today, although the excavations of Luciana Jacobelli in 1990 found no flooring and no masonry.[12] There are believed to have been other structures here, however, probably linked to the cult, given the very large quantity of finds in what was a fairly limited part of the site, subsequently destroyed by the construction of the tower. The crypto-portico visible today on the first terrace, open towards the south, served to support and expand the upper level. Indeed, the Roman concrete discovered on the east

Analysis of the context 61

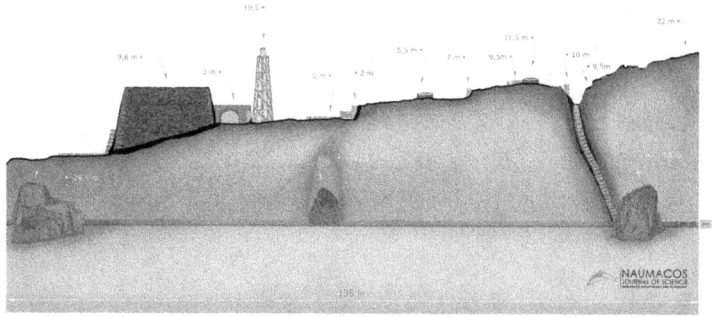

Figure 6.10 Perspective section of Punta Campanella. The lines of the terraces are shown through the preserved boundaries and the eastern flight of steps carved in the rock.

Credit: Naumacos – Gabriele Gomez de Ayala.

side of the first terrace seems to have completely closed off the crypto-portico at that end and filled the space between the structure and the cliff edge. Given the broad flat space resulting from this arrangement, the second terrace is thus believed to have hosted a portico, perhaps with colonnades in an 'L' or 'U' shape, as in the case of the temple of Venus in Pompeii in the 2nd century BC,[13] open towards the sea. On the next terrace up, there may thus have been a sacellum for the cult, as well as privileged access to the cave below via the steps carved into the rocky cleft. Indeed, it is only the third and final terrace that provides a clear view in all directions of both gulfs.

In advance of future archaeological research that may clarify the nature of the complex, this reading thus indicates a sanctuary arranged over terraces (Figure 6.10), of which today the access road and lower and upper porticoes probably remain.

On the basis, then, of a preliminary reconstruction, the sanctuary in the territory of Surrentum in its Hellenistic phase, i.e., the 3rd or more likely the 2nd century BC, is consistent with other Hellenistic Italic sanctuaries in the central Italic area.[14] The capital with birds on the corners may belong to the portico or another building if it is indeed from Punta Campanella. Ahead of its precise chronological and typological characterisation,[15] the acanthus leaves of the crown are clearly of the Augustan period.

Traces of occupation in the Roman period, from the 1st century BC onwards, were not found, although the refurbishment of the area near the road could, in theory, be attributed to this phase. The presence, known only from the literature, of *opus reticulatum* along the steps leading down to the cave on the eastern side might indicate that it was rebuilt in the early imperial epoch. It should also be remembered that the area of the sanctuary was still visible to

Figure 6.11 Massa Lubrense, archaeological storage. Roman inscription from surveys at Punta Campanella.

Credit: Author.

Strabo and subsequently Statius. In addition, the *Tabula Peutingeriana*, datable to the 4th century AD,[16] makes explicit reference to the presence of a *templum Minervae* at the tip of the peninsula, beyond the city of Surrentum. The continuity of use of the sanctuary might be indicated by the random discovery of a small fragment of a marble epigraph (Figure 6.11) that reads:

[C]n(aeus) Hegi[us –]vus IIII[vir].

Hegius, a name of Oscan origin attested only in Pompeii,[17] was probably a *quattuorvir* (magistrate) in Surrentum. The inscription, dated to the last few decades of the 1st century BC, has a clear votive character, the magistrate dedicating in the sanctuary a small ex-voto with his name on it.

Notes

1 W. Johannowky, in *Culti della Campania antica* 1998, 287. Actually, some doubts also emerged in the discussion at the 1991 conference, for which see *Discussione*, in *Campanella* 1992, 239–241.
2 Mingazzini, Pfister 1946, 143.
3 Mingazzini, Pfister 1946, 143–147, strongly supported the thesis that a Roman villa had been established on the promontory of Punta Campanella, which would have spared, however, the temple. The authors placed the temple on the terrace where the mediaeval tower was built, while the villa would have been built on the remaining area, although the temple, as will be seen, is attested until late antiquity.
4 On the development of this type of structure, see Giuliani 1973.
5 The dating of the colonnade has been the subject of debate in recent years. It is attributed to the 2nd century BC by de Waele 2001, 332, and instead dated to the Neronian age after investigations by University of Rome "La Sapienza", for which, see D'Alessio 2009, 31, with bibliography. Differently, Wolf 2009, 289, refers the portico to the late Samnite period, whose restoration from the foundations in the Neronian period he then proposes. Recently, clarify the dating Osanna, Giletti 2020; Osanna, Gerogiannis, Giletti 2021.
6 Triantafillis 2014. On this topic, see Adinolfi, Senatore 2015.
7 De Angelis d'Ossat 1977. Among the latter, see Di Luca 2009, who, however, places, erroneously in my opinion, the construction of the villa at the end of the 1st century BC.
8 It is possible to refer to the comparisons of Giuliani 1973.
9 For the part of the substructure with smaller splinters, see the bridge of the Via Appia over the Vallumana ditch (Quilici 2002, 141–142, 2004, 457–458) and, for the part with larger and better shaped splinters, compare the substructure, possibly also of the Via Appia, at Masseria di Val Maiuri (Quilici 2004, 457). In Campania, see a polygonal substructure in the section of the Via Appia near Sinuessa, in the Triglione di Mondragone district, for which, see Cascella 2017, 39–40, fig. 29 (dated between the 2nd and 1st century BC). Comparisons with the masonry techniques of Latium and those of the Via Appia are numerous, but those indicated seem the most pertinent. In any case, an accurate study of wall stratigraphy will be necessary to determine, above all, relative chronologies of the Via Minervia, since the autopsy analysis of the facing in itself is not probative but only indicative.
10 Teresa Caputo (Caputo 2004, 83) dates the limestone *opus incertum* of the Via Minervia substructures to the imperial period, following the suggestion of the presence of an imperial villa on Punta Campanella.
11 See Adinolfi, Senatore 2015, 280 and *passim*, for synthesis of dating theories.
12 Jacobelli 1994.
13 On the Venus temple of Pompeii, see D'Alessio 2009, 39–40. For the recent excavations, see Battiloro, Mogetta 2021.
14 A lucid analysis of these contexts is in D'Alessio 2011 (with bibliography).
15 On the figured capitals with owls, see von Mercklin 1962, 237–238, dated in the known cases no earlier than the Augustan Age. For the capital in the Museo Archeologico Territoriale della Penisola Sorrentina "G. Vallet", which is very peculiar and unique, an in-depth study will have to be carried out to understand its style, dating and significance.
16 Prontera 2003.
17 See Salomies 2012, 154.

7 Chronological phases and clues to the nature of the cult

The study presented here has sought to summarise the constitutive elements, from the historical, archaeological and cult point of view, of the territory of Surrentum. What emerges is an extremely complex and stratified situation in terms of both the arrangement of the buildings and the cult itself. There is no doubt that the myth of the Sirens and the cult of Athena characterised this region and represented a key part of its identity up until the Roman epoch.[1]

According to the literary sources, in the region of Surrentum,[2] the promontory at the tip of the peninsula was occupied by the Sirens[3] before the *nostos* of the heroes of the Trojan War. Ulysses encountered them here during his long journey back to Ithaca, but the most recent studies[4] of the mythical geography of his journey, as established by Greek colonists, identify the Sirens with the three small islands today called Li Galli, near the Sorrentine Peninsula but on the Salerno side.[5] While we can be certain of the location of these female-headed monsters – and their 'tomb', arising from petrification[6] – reports of a cult, and, thus, a sanctuary, are much more problematic. Citing Timaeus, Pseudo-Aristotle speaks only of the sanctuary of the Sirens, which he claimed stood on the promontory enclosing the Bay of Ieranto, further to the east and closer to Li Galli.[7] In contrast, regarding Punta Campanella, the sources concur on the existence of the temple of Athena. Writing in the Augustan period, Strabo attributes the creation of the sanctuary to Ulysses,[8] and although initially he places the temple of the Sirens on the previously mentioned islands and the sanctuary of Athena on the cape, in the next passage, he alludes to a superimposition of the two cults, as does Pliny the Elder subsequently.[9] Statius, in contrast, stresses the importance of the cult of Athena and its rituals, including a libation of wine poured into the sea, indirectly implying that this was the custom among those who passed through the strait between the Cape and the island of Capri.[10] As late as 172 BC, the Roman Senate decreed the expiation of the *prodigia* – a lightning bolt that struck the *Columna Rostrata* erected in 245 BC – by sending a delegation to the sanctuary.[11]

The question of the sanctuary of the Sirens has obviously been widely discussed in the literature by Mingazzini (who identifies it with the Bay of Ieranto),[12] Beloch,[13] Emanuele Greco,[14] Bruno d'Agostino[15] and Luisa Breglia

DOI: 10.4324/9781032647548-7

Chronological phases and clues to the nature of the cult 65

Pulci Doria,[16] who, together with Mario Russo,[17] locates it closer to Naples.[18] There has also been much debate over the years as to whether the cult of Athena was practised in the sacred area of Punta Campanella from its foundation or was superimposed on the earlier cult of the Sirens.[19]

Wherever the primitive cult of the Sirens is located, it is closely connected to Greek colonisation. As clarified by Alfonso Mele,[20] the Sorrentine Sirens differ from those of the Greek literary tradition. The name of Parthenope, the Siren who died in the place where the city named after her was later founded by colonists from Cumae and whose cult would subsequently be revived in the polyadic rites of Neapolis, evokes the role played by the cult in the social transition of a woman from maiden to bride. The death of the Sirens, caused by the goddesses of love and marriage, Aphrodite and Hera, marks a woman's rebirth in her new social status. Thus, the original cult of Parthenope, established and developed in the Sorrentine sanctuary in the course of the 8th and 7th centuries BC and centred on rites of passage, was characterised by a Euboean dimension that had nothing to do with the journeys of Ulysses.[21] There is no doubt that from the Archaic period onwards, the myth of the Sirens formed part of the identity of the inhabitants of the Sorrentine Peninsula, and it is frequently seen in their figured ceramics. An example is a small amphora produced in Chalcis discovered in the necropolis of Sant'Agata sui Due Golfi (Figure 7.1),[22] not far from Punta Campanella, and a *lekane* produced in Campania from the necropolis of the Hotel Vittoria in Sorrento (Figure 7.2).[23]

Figure 7.1 Piano di Sorrento, Museo Archeologico Territoriale "G. Vallet". Chalcidian amphora with Siren from the necropolis of Sant'Agata sui Due Golfi.

Credit: Author.

Figure 7.2 Sorrento, Museo Correale di Terranova. Pyxis with Siren from the necropolis of Hotel Vittoria.

Credit: Teresa Laudonia photograph.

Given the current state of the research, it is not known whether the sanctuary of the Sirens was situated at Punta Campanella, when it originated or when it fell into decline. Although the site was probably frequented by indigenous groups in the preceding period, the sanctuary of Punta Campanella was founded in the second half of the 6th century BC.[24] The first temple building may be attributed to this phase, attested by simas with lion-head protomes of Achaean-Posidonian influence.[25] The most ancient archaeological evidence of the cult points to some female divinity, highlighted by a large number of protomes and busts with *poloi* of the late-Archaic period. Characterised by elongated oval faces of the Ionic type with the hint of an Archaic smile and a flattened nose, they are all fractured just above the eyebrows (Figure 7.3).

On the basis of comparisons with other sanctuary contexts in southern Italy, especially the area of Posidonia, they can be dated to the late-Archaic period (late 6th and early 5th centuries).[26]

Also attributed to the late 5th or 4th century BC is a refurbishment of the cult buildings, attested by residues of the architectural decoration, which is consistent with other regional evidence reflecting a revival of Archaic sanctuaries under the influence of Neapolis.[27] Of interest are the fragments of nimbate antefixes, again dated to the late 5th century BC.

To the period from the second half of the 4th to the 2nd centuries BC[28] are dated numerous terracotta statuettes showing Athena with the Phrygian helmet, broadly similar despite belonging to chronologically successive types, perhaps because they were inspired by a cult statue.[29] Mario Russo recognised nine variants,[30] all with a *patera* in the right hand and shield in the left

Figure 7.3 Massa Lubrense, archaeological storage. Fragments of late archaic heads.
Credit: Author.

(Figure 7.4, coll. Fluss), which are also present, albeit with some differences, in Pompeii, Stabiae (Privati district) and Posidonia.[31]

However, the debate over the representation of the goddess needs to be investigated further on the basis of the real distinctions detectable in the facial features and the absence or presence of distinctive elements on the helmet, as well as differences in production technique. Indeed, a large group of specimens produced by joining two moulds, with subsequent processing by hand using specific tools, in which the face is rendered very simply with only the significant features, is usually dated to the mid 4th century.[32] However, other heads are less standardised and the helmet is rendered more sharply (Figure 7.5), and these appear to be older, possibly from the 5th century BC. Slightly more recent than these are other heads with more voluminous hair and a by-then simplified helmet (Figure 7.6).

Other votive objects, such as the statuettes of *kourotrophoi* of the 4th-3rd centuries BC (Figure 7.7),[33] appear complementary, referencing the sphere of female fertility, and are widely attested in sets of votive objects in southern Italy.[34]

68 *Chronological phases and clues to the nature of the cult*

Figure 7.4 Massa Lubrense, archaeological storage. Statuette of Athena Ilias from Fluss collection.

Credit: Soprintendenza Archive.

Figure 7.5 Piano di Sorrento, Museo Archeologico Territoriale "G. Vallet". Head of Athena Ilias.

Credit: Author.

Chronological phases and clues to the nature of the cult 69

Figure 7.6 Massa Lubrense, archaeological storage. Fragments of Athena Ilias heads.
Credit: Author.

Figure 7.7 Massa Lubrense, archaeological storage. Fragments of *kourotrophos* figurines.
Credit: Author.

The same theme is recalled by three headless and limbless fragments of female bodies wearing a *chiton* puffed-up on the belly, comparable with specimens from the Privati district, to be interpreted as figures of pregnant women.[35] A highly standardised model of female figures circulating in southern Italy and

70 *Chronological phases and clues to the nature of the cult*

Figure 7.8 Massa Lubrense, archaeological storage. Fragments of a Hellenistic head.
Credit: Author.

Sicily is exemplified by the so-called Tanagrines, attested by numerous heads with hair in the "melon" style with the addition of earrings, together with anatomic fragments and rare traces of polychromatic decoration (Figure 7.8).

Once again, it is possible to see a strong affinity with the nearby sanctuaries of *Stabiae* and the area of Pompeii, where the same types of votive objects are found together.[36]

The large corpus of small figures includes nude male bodies, headless and limbless, some with a slight hint of a mantle, and a torso of a seated child, again comparable with the votive deposit of Privati, also linked to the theme of fertility, as are the rare fragments of infants' faces.[37] Some heads can also be assimilated into small erotes, similar to specimens from the Temple of Apollo in Pompeii and the votive deposit in the Bottaro district, which have been interpreted as being linked to processions in honour of Aphrodite and Bacchus.[38]

Figure 7.9 Massa Lubrense, archaeological storage. Fragments of a female head with polos.

Credit: Author.

Of great importance are the protomes, with *poloi* dated to the late 5th and 4th centuries BC[39]: they have wavy hair on the forehead (Figures 7.9–7.10), of clear Siceliote influence,[40] widely attested in the Gulf of Naples in Stabiae, Pompeii and *Neapolis*.[41]

At Punta Campanella, we may thus recognise without doubt the sanctuary of Athena, who appears in both the coroplastic art and red-figure vessels (Figure 7.11).

In the organisation of the cult in the 6th and 5th centuries BC, the role first of Cumae and then of Neapolis was decisive,[42] especially in their territorial policies. Neapolis was founded in the last quarter of the 6th century BC by colonists from Cumae.[43] The relationship of the Greek cities of Cumae and Neapolis,[44] but also Posidonia (founded at the end of the 7th century BC), with the Etruscan and Italic components of Campania, strongly rooted in this region, was thus highly important. Also important was the position of the city of Surrentum, in whose territory the sanctuary of Athena was founded.[45]

72 *Chronological phases and clues to the nature of the cult*

Figure 7.10 Massa Lubrense, archaeological storage. Fragments of a female head with polos.

Credit: Author.

Figure 7.11 Massa Lubrense, storage. Fragments of a red-figure vase with Athena.

Credit: Author.

In about 450 BC, Athens established its hegemony over the region, attested in the Gulf by the offering made to the Siren Parthenope by the general Diotimos.[46] In addition to Athens,[47] the dissemination of the cult of Athena in the 6th and 5th centuries BC reflected the political influence of other Greek cities operating in the Tyrrhenian Sea in that period, such as Rhodes.[48]

On the basis of the currently available evidence, it could be argued that the cult of Athena[49] existed in the region from the mid-6th century BC onwards,[50] but it is not known whether the goddess was already by then characterised as Ilias,[51] as was the case in Posidonia.[52] In addition, the cult of Athena reflects a colonial dimension regarding this region that dates back to the mythical age of Ulysses[53] and finds other outlets[54] among the landings along the Sorrentine Peninsula and, thus, along the coastal maritime routes to Stabiae and Pompeii.[55] Similar phenomena are seen in Puglia, with Artemis Bendis[56] along the Ionian coast and Athena again along the Adriatic.[57] However, cults of Athena have also been reported over the centuries in the Gulf of Salerno, where votive objects associated with Athena Ilias are also found, for example, on Agropoli, the promontory that marks the boundary of the territory of Posidonia,[58] as well as in the latter city itself, in the *Athenaion* of the so-called *Tempio di Cerere*.[59] Moreover, Athena with the epiclesis Ilias recalls the Palladion, the cult sculpture of the temple of the goddess in Ilion (Troy), stolen by the Achaeans, specifically Diomedes. It thus constitutes a direct reference for Hellenic peoples to the role played by the *poleis* in foreign lands, which the Sorrentine Peninsula definitely was. For this reason, it is possible to hypothesise the spread of a cult of Athena Ilias, with expressly Greek traits, from the late 5th century BC onwards.[60] The regional spread of a coastal cult of Athena reflects Greek occupation, which in the course of the 5th century BC saw the establishment of an equilibrium between Posidonia, Cumae and Neapolis.[61]

The recent discovery of another important maritime sanctuary on the coast of the Salento peninsula, near what the literary sources call *Castrum Minervae*, identified with the modern Castro (LE),[62] has undoubtedly reopened the debate over the importance of the cult of Athena Ilias. Indeed, a cult statue of the late 4th century BC, carved in Taras from local stone (*pietra tenera*), replicates the iconography seen on a bronze statuette also discovered in the area. It consists of Athena wearing a sleeveless chiton with no aegis, holding a shield in her lowered left hand and a spear in her right, while on her head, she wears a helmet with a distinctive forward-tilted apex, typical of Phrygia. Following an indigenous occupation in the 8th and 7th centuries BC, the sanctuary of Castro was established in the second half of the 6th century BC. Some architectural decoration produced in Taras and an altar with a hole drilled through it used for the cult of chthonian divinities remain of this early phase. In contrast, a monumental acrolith in Cycladic marble and completed in wood, which represents, as ably reconstructed by Francesco D'Andria, an early cult statue of Athena, perhaps produced in Athens, is dated to the last third of the 5th century BC. The two sanctuaries thus appear to have much in common, including their strategic function of marking the entrance to the

Greek territories of Taras in one case and Cumae/Neapolis in the other. As shown by the cult statue and the corresponding votive material, both adopted the cult of Athena[63] in the 5th century BC at the latest, perhaps in the form of Ilias from the very start but certainly by the end of the 4th century BC. Further evidence of the close correspondence of the cults is provided by the discovery in the excavations of Castro of a head in terracotta of a type widely attested in Campania and Punta Campanella in particular. Even the clay of which it is made, in macroscopic terms, seems to indicate that it was produced in Campania.[64] In fact, the sources hint at relations between Taras and Neapolis – and thus Surrentum – precisely at the end of the 4th century BC.[65] In the Aeneid, it is to the Athena of Castro that the Trojans, led by Aeneas, offered their first sacrifices on arriving in Italy,[66] and there may be a connection with Dionysius of Halicarnassus' account of a possible sacrifice in the Tyrrhenian area, perhaps precisely at Punta Campanella.[67]

From a ritual point of view, the cult of Athena shared many characteristics with that of the Sirens[68]: the goddess is associated with a state of virginity, a divine *nymphe* and patron of human *nymphai*,[69] and for this reason, together with other divinities of the Greek *pantheon*, she is part of female rituals accompanying a change of status, in this case, linked to the education and preparation of young women with regard to sexuality.[70] The prevalent female nature[71] of the cult is also shown by the presence of votive objects recalling aspects of the female socio-economic sphere, such as spinning, marking the goddess as the patron of handicrafts,[72] but also by the previously mentioned *kourotrophoi* and other objects linked to fertility that, especially in the Hellenistic period, are also directed towards the male sphere (erotes, children, etc.).[73] Other materials with female connotations found in abundance include the miniature *kantharoi* (Figure 7.12) found in the extra-urban female sanctuaries of southern Italy, especially near sources of water, inside votive deposits and buried upside-down in the ground.[74]

In the case of the small containers from Punta Campanella, a small percentage of specimens present traces of burning, perhaps linked to selective rituals for the combustion of small quantities of food.[75]

It is in this sense that the votive offerings of busts and fictile protomes with *poloi*, of both the Archaic and Classical epochs, can be interpreted. Widely documented in other coeval contexts in Magna Graecia and Sicily, they allude strongly, as demonstrated by Elisa Chiara Portale,[76] to the *nymphai*. The rituals associated with the cult of Athena Ilias in southern Italy, as described by Lycophron, for example, in Daunia and Locri, from which maidens were sent to the sanctuary of Athena in Troy,[77] involved girls embracing the cult statue, just as Cassandra did during the Trojan War. This enables us to hypothesise that the cult of Athena at Punta Campanella also had an initiatory function in the female sphere, linked to changes in status: the *parthenoi* 'temporarily' follow the example of Cassandra in her 'denied marriage', before acquiring the status of *nymphai*.[78]

Chronological phases and clues to the nature of the cult 75

Figure 7.12 Massa Lubrense, storage. Group of miniature votive cups.
Credit: Author.

In this sense, the interpretation of the eastern steps leading down to the Bay of Ieranto might be important. As we have seen, they lead down to a small karst cave and not a landing. In the ancient world, especially in Greece, caves were perceived as thresholds at the boundary between different worlds, where initiatory rituals linked to the change in status[79] from adolescence to adulthood were practised. In this context, Pan was frequently associated with nymphs[80] as they participated in prenuptial rituals linked to the female sphere.[81] Indeed, the caves hosted rituals in which girls were initiated to the stage of *nymphai* via the purifying power of water.[82] The most famous example of the association between caves and the sanctuaries of Athena was in Lindos on the island of Rhodes.[83] Here, beneath the temple of the acropolis, whose original Archaic layout was monumentalised in the Hellenistic period, there is a large cave accessible from the summit of the sanctuary, which was the centre of a cult attested by votive materials discovered inside it.[84] In addition, it has been suggested that the floor of the temple on the island of Rhodes was left unpaved in order to maintain the link with the natural rock and thus with the cave below. In this sense, rock is fundamental to the sacral nature of the site.[85] The tradition of the foundation of Parthenope by colonists from Rhodes is known from the sources, but it is also useful here to highlight the link between the cult of Athena in Lindos and that of Syracuse.[86] Returning to the Sorrentine Peninsula, recent investigations have revealed the presence, inside the sanctuary linked to the Triangular Forum in Pompeii, plausibly attributable to

Athena/Minerva, of two caves used for cult practices that were obliterated in the late 2nd century BC.[87]

Regarding the meaning of Athena along the coasts, she was considered to be the patron of sailors, Ulysses first and foremost,[88] and the goddess of *metis*, i.e., wisdom.[89] This aspect was not secondary but is related to the multiple vocations typical of frontier sanctuaries and especially a *polymetis* and polysemic divinity such as Athena.[90] Of the many cases, given their position near the sea and their traditional link to navigation, the sanctuaries of Athena Lindia in Rhodes and Athena Sounia in Attica are emblematic in this regard.[91]

In a certain period, perhaps as early as the second half of the 4th century BC or shortly afterwards, the sanctuary fell within the Samnite sphere of influence. This is shown by the reference to Nocera, Pompeii and Surrentum in the names of the colonies instituted by the Nucerian P. Sittio, i.e. *Sarnensis*, *Veneria* and *Minervia*, but also by the inscription that refers to the *meddices Menervii*, still of uncertain dating (between the early 3rd and the early 2nd centuries BC).[92] To the late 4th or early 3rd century BC may be dated the urban layout of Surrentum and probably the building of the first stretch of the Via Minervia,[93] while a refurbishment of the architectural decorations, with protome antefixes of Athena Ilias, may be dated to the second half of the 4th century BC. The latter are also seen in other cities of the Nucerine League,[94] but above all they are present in the sanctuaries of Privati and Pompeii, closely connected to the Sorrentine *Athenaion*.[95] In votive terms, at Punta Campanella, statuettes of Tanagrines and dancers with the 'melon' hairstyle, as well as of Athena Ilias, are widely attested.

Notes

1 On the topic very important is Breglia 2016.
2 The sources are well summarised and analysed in Breglia Pulci Doria 1996.
3 For a comprehensive analysis of the Sirens, see Breglia Pulci Doria 1987. On the relationship between Sirens and Athena linked to the sea: Breglia Pulci Doria 1992. See also the careful analyses of Federico 2010a; Mele 2016; Senatore 2020. Also important are Breglia Pulci Doria 1990, 1995; Senatore 2014; Breglia 2016. A useful and incisive summary is in Giampaola, Greco 2022.
4 The book of Braccesi (2010) is the most important recent study on this topic.
5 Federico 2010a; Mele 2014, 151–171 clarifies in detail the ideological and cultic construction of the Sorrentine Sirens' myth, which refers to the second half of the 7th century BC, and the Tyrrhenian localisation process of Ulysses' journey.
6 Federico 2010a, 2010b.
7 Pseudo-Aristotle, *De mirab.*, 103.
8 Strab., V, 4, 8.
9 Plin., *Nat.* III, 62. Both use the same source, Artemidorus, see Greco 1992.
10 Stat., *Silv.* III, 2, 23.
11 Liv., XLII, 20.
12 Mingazzini, Pfister 1946, 17, 45–50, 51–53, 83–84.
13 Beloch 1989, 293, places it at Marina della Lobra.
14 Greco 1992, proposes locating the sanctuary of the Sirens towards *Aequa* and perhaps in the Trinità district in Piano di Sorrento; see also Greco 1995.

15 d'Agostino 1992 places it on Monte S. Costanzo.
16 Breglia Pulci Doria 1995, 29, proposed the Deserto district in the hamlet of Sant'Agata sui Due Golfi in Massa Lubrense.
17 Russo 1998, 59–62, also thinks about Trinità district in Piano di Sorrento.
18 Pais 1908 first located the sanctuary of the Sirens in Massa Lubrense, Naples side.
19 Already Russo 1990, 256, thinks that Athena was preceded by a chthonic deity, later identified with the Sirens. Breglia Pulci Doria 1992; Breglia 2016, 4–8, speaks in the sense of an overlapping of the cult. d'Agostino 1992 (followed by Breglia Pulci Doria 1995, 29) argues with great acumen the overlapping witnessed by Strabo in terms of a different chronology of traditions that, inevitably, merge with time. Greco 1992, 1995 distinguishes the two sanctuaries and ascribes an overlap to the sources. Carafa 2008, 14, then alludes to an early overlap between Sirens and Athena. Mele 2014, 152, 171, argues that the promontory was characterised by the more ancient cult of the Sirens, which was replaced by that of Athena in the 6th century BC. Mele 2016, 289, 297–299, associates the creation of the temples of the Sirens and Athena with the phase of urban structuring of Sorrento, thus with the second half of the 6th century BC, without speaking of an overlapping but rather of their coexistence. Most recently, Cerchiai 2017 argued that the sanctuary of the Sirens coexisted with that of Athena.
20 Mele 2014, 158–159, 2016, 314–315. This reading is later developed by Breglia 2016, 4–8. The mythical tradition of the Sirens of Sorrento and Parthenope, in particular, "segue una strada autonoma", in the words of Alfonso Mele. Mele 2014, 170, also emphasises the role of Cumae in structuring the cult of the Sirens.
21 These clues are very effectively clarified by Mele 2016. For another implication more related to the chthonic and liminal meaning, see Breglia Pulci Doria 1990; Carafa 2008, 12–13.
22 Puglia 2016.
23 Laudonia 2013.
24 This has been argued recently by Mele 2014, 152.
25 Rescigno 2010, 185–186; Mele 2016, 289, rightly argues for an influence of Posidonia in the creation (in the 6th century BC) of the sanctuary of Athena on the promontory, at a stage coinciding with the urban structuring of Sorrento.
26 We find them in the extraurban zone of Posidonia and generally in areas of Achaean influence (see Ferrara 2009, 106, no. 274).
27 Rescigno 1998, 2010, 188.
28 It cannot be ruled out at the moment that some finds point to a higher date, at least to the second half of the 5th century BC, such as the head reproduced in Figure 7.5. More in-depth studies will be needed to clarify this. As for the chronology of the statuettes, scholars have always agreed that the production of these statuettes began in the second half of the 4th century and reached the first half of the 2nd century BC (Russo 1990, nos. 343–383, 235–239, 255), as well as in Stabiae (Miniero 2002, 20); while in the Poseidonian sphere, the elaboration of the type should be backdated by about a century (Cipriani 2002, 43–44; Cipriani, Avagliano 2005).
29 On the recurrence of the Athena with Phrygian helmet in sculptures in the round and elsewhere, see Laubscher 1980. Torelli 2002 rightly questions the actual correspondence between the image of Athena Ilias, known from the antefix but also from the coroplastic figures, and the corresponding cult. One of the best heads of Athena Ilias from Punta Campanella is reproduced in Figure 7.5: belonging to the Anastasio collection and published in Russo 1992, 238, no. 366, tav. XLI, it is now in the Museo Archeologico Territoriale della Penisola Sorrentina "G. Vallet".
30 The variants proposed by Russo differ essentially in the position of the head, or for small differences in the face.
31 Parisi 2017, 192–194, fig. 9, with a timely summary of the previous bibliography.
32 There are 134 finds, to be divided between complete heads and separate moulds.

78 *Chronological phases and clues to the nature of the cult*

33 Breglia Pulci Doria 1998 argues the cult of Athena in the sense of *kourotrophos*, linking it to an Athenian influence.
34 Parisi 2017, 189.
35 Miniero 2002, 23–24.
36 Miniero 2002, 22; Parisi 2017.
37 Miniero et al. 1997, 39, no. 3.
38 Parisi 2017, 194–195.
39 This typology, attested in many sanctuaries, has been well developed by Elisa Chiara Portale from a semantic point of view in the sense of representing *nymphai*, for which see *infra*.
40 Portale 2012a, 2012b.
41 For Pompei (Parisi 2017, 168–187; Osanna 2017, 83); for Stabiae (Miniero 2002, 24, fig. 21); for Neapolis (De Simone, Borriello 1985, 162–163). On the spread of the type, see Greco 2017, 170–171.
42 Giangiulio 1986, 135, proposes its creation at the orbit of Cumae. Greco 1992; De Caro 1992 supported the hypothesis of an influence of Neapolis on Punta Campanella from an advanced phase, namely the end of the 4th century BC. The reading that I believe to be most effective in political terms was provided by Breglia Pulci Doria 1998, who states that a Chalcidian matrix of Cumae (partly already in Breglia Pulci Doria 1995) in the creation of the sanctuary would have been succeeded by a Neapolitan influence – under Athenian pressure – during the 5th century BC. This would also be partly supported by the presence of a Chalcidian amphora and other material of the same matrix in the indigenous necropolis of Sant'Agata sui Due Golfi, see Sampaolo 1992a; Mele 2016 also reads the Hellenic policy against the Etruscanisation of Campania very well. An archaeological reading from Pompeii to the Sorrentine Peninsula of this period is now offered by Osanna, Rescigno 2021. Finally, see the useful historical-archaeological framing of the Sorrentine Peninsula and its cults from a Cumaean perspective by Greco 2021a.
43 Breglia Pulci Doria 1995, 1998, 103–106, reads in Strabo's passage, in which he mentions a foundation of the sanctuary by Ulysses, a Chalcidian – and thus Aristodemus of Cumae – component in the creation of the sanctuary; at the meantime in Diodorus Sicuro's passage on Liparus and Aeolus. On Liparus and his cult, see Mele 2016.
44 There is a vast bibliography on these topics. See, especially for what is important here, the relationship between Cumae and Neapolis after its foundation, and for this, see Mele 2009, 2014, 141–213.
45 Mele 2016 reflects on these issues with great insight, to which we refer for the diachronic political structuring of cults in the territory of Surrentum. This is how one reads the contrast between Hellenic and Italic, first Etruscan and then Samnite communities.
46 For the Athenian presence and especially of Diotimos in Neapolis, see Maurizi 1993–95, 296–304; Mele 2007, 259–261.
47 Breglia Pulci Doria 1992, 1998.
48 Pugliese Carratelli 1990, 275; Maddoli 1991, 247–249, hypothesised a cult established by the Rhodians.
49 The characterisation of the Punta Campanella's Athena as it appears from the coroplastic art was not immediately clear. Zancani Montuoro 1990 spoke of a derivation from the Athenian Parthenos, due to the presence of the shield and helmet. It was De Caro 1992 who recognised a Phrygian or Trojan Athena, by virtue of the particular shape of the helmet, emphasising the recurrence of the type also in two other important sanctuaries, at Stabiae in the Privati sanctuary and at Pompeii in the Triangular Forum. He, however, in recognising the image of the Athena of Troy for the first time, saw in it a distant reference to the foundation myth of Ulysses and a desire

on the part of the Samnites to structure noble origins by introducing an illustrious antecedent in this territory, under the influence of Rome (followed, among others, by Scatozza Höricht 1997; Torelli 2002). Recently, this hypothesis has been rightly questioned by Carafa 2008, 14, who also argues that the Sorrento sanctuary is not mentioned as Athena Ilias by Strabo, who lists Siris, Rome, Lanuvio and Luceria as places of worship of the goddess. However, it should be pointed out that the sanctuary of Castro is also not indicated by Strabo, for which see *infra*. Greco 1992 and Guzzo 1992 are in agreement in placing the cult of Athena in the late 4th century BC. The topic was then dealt with at length in various contributions in the proceedings of the conference *Elmo frigio* 2002. In particular, Breglia Pulci Doria 1995, 39–42, 1998, 2002, 131–132, considers that the "marine" and curotrophic Athena in the Classical period would have been flanked by the image of Phrygian Athena in the late 4th century BC. Cerchiai 2002 argues for the importance of Capua in the spread of Athena's image with Phrygian helmet, also in the 4th century BC.

50 It was first Breglia Pulci Doria 1998, in her comprehensive review of the cult of the sanctuary of Punta Campanella, who pointed out the existence of a Greek cult as early as the 6th century BC, proposing precisely an Athena in a "marine" and then "curotrophic" sense. According to the author (already in Breglia Pulci Doria 1995), from a historical point of view, the cult of the Archaic period would have had a Chalcidian influence and would be reflected in Strabo's passage alluding to Ulysses but also in Diodorus Sicurus' passage on Liparus and Aeolus. Mele 2014, 152, 2016, 289, reiterates the development of the cult of Athena in the 6th century BC. It is worth noting that recent research in the Trianglular Forum of Pompeii suggests that a cult of Athena was already present in the 6th century BC, see Osanna 2017.

51 On the spread of the cult of Athena Ilias in Italy, see Breglia Pulci Doria 2002, 120–131.

52 In fact, it is important to note that the first cult at Posidonia, at least from the end of the 6th century BC onwards, is characterised in its meaning of Athena Ilias and persisted into the 5th century and beyond, see Cipriani 2002. Mele 2016, 289, not surprisingly argues for an influence of Posidonia in the creation of Athena's sanctuary at Punta Campanella.

53 As supported by Breglia Pulci Doria 1998.

54 De Caro 1992, 174, admits a dependence of the sanctuaries of Privati in Stabiae and the Triangular Forum in Pompeii on that of Punta Campanella.

55 D'Alessio 2009, 112, had already suggested a connection to the sea of these three sanctuaries in Campania. An overview of the landings on the Peninsula, certainly to be further investigated, is offered by Bonghi Jovino 2008. In fact, the layout of the sanctuary in Pompeii is coeval with that of Punta Campanella, while the one in Stabiae, as far as is known, is more recent, dating at the earliest to the end of the 5th century BC.

56 Mancini 2020, 55–56, with bibliography.

57 D'Andria 2020.

58 Fiammenghi 1985.

59 Cipriani 2002; Cipriani, Avagliano 2005.

60 In such a political key, one can mention the theory of Mugione 2002 (followed by Torelli 2002), who ascribes the development of the Athena Ilias' iconography on Apulian vases to the end of the 5th century BC and an allusion to victory, recalling the cult of Athena *Skyletria* mentioned by Lycophron near Tarentum, i.e., Castro (*Alexandra*, v. 853). As D'Andria 2020, 131 points out, the cult of Athena Ilias would have been brought to the sanctuary of Castro from Taras, in the context of a domination of the Ionian Gulf, from the end of the 5th century BC. The example of Taras, with the important discovery of the Castro sanctuary and its various implications for the spread of the Athena Ilias' image, is undoubtedly diriment in

the context of Punta Campanella. Here, therefore, a Samnite or Roman matrix at the origin of the cult of Athena Ilias, which has a clear Greek imprint, is not supported, as argued by other authors before.

61 Rescigno 2010, 183; Rescigno 2020.
62 Most recently D'Andria 2020. A complete analysis of the excavations and objects is now *Athenaion* 2023.
63 Torelli 2002 rightly emphasises the construction of the Athena Ilias' image in the Taras area as early as the end of the 5th century BC. For this, see the analysis of Apulian ceramics in Mugione 2002.
64 D'Andria 2020, 116, fig. 39.
65 Breglia Pulci Doria 1996, 175–176; Torelli 2002 not surprisingly emphasises the importance of Taras in the development of the Athena Ilias' iconography from the end of the 5th century BC.
66 Verg., *Aen.* III, 530–546.
67 On this hypothesis, see Cerchiai 2002, 33–35.
68 Already Carafa 2008, 14, disagrees on a political component linked to Rome and the Samnites and perceives in the cult of Athena Ilias a rituality in the transitions of women's status. D'Alessio 2009, 112, identifies in the characteristics of the archaic Athena of Pompeii (which she links to the goddess worshipped at Punta Campanella) the traits of a peaceful goddess, linked to female reproduction and the chthonic aspect. The latter component, however, would have been overcome in the Samnite age, following a direction more closely linked to craftsmanship and the healthy sphere. In reality, these aspects, as will be seen, are complementary. Breglia 2016, 4–8, reads a change in the name of the promontory of Punta Campanella and a possible subordination of the Sirens to Athena. For a semantic assimilation between Sirens (and also owls) and Athena in terms of a rituality of passage, particularly expressed in Campania, see Mancini 2007.
69 On the term *nymphe* as a maiden of marriageable age, see Andò 1996.
70 See, for instance, the Athenian festivities of the *arrephorae*, for which see also on an archaeological level Cruccas 2007 (with bibliography) and Håland 2012 (for the connection with agriculture). See also, for the role of Athena in the construction of the ancient woman in her relationship with Hera and Aphrodite, Menichetti 2006. In general, see Larson 2001, 100–120; Ferrari 2003, 2004. See also an interesting vase by the Dolone Painter with Athena at the spring, with votive statues in the background, Menichetti 2006. On the rituals, in the Greek and Magna Graecia worlds, concerning passages of status and the importance of such a cult within sanctuaries, the bibliography is extremely varied.
71 Russo 1990, 256, and Breglia Pulci Doria 2002, 132, had already timidly put forward a hypothesis in the sense of a fertility-related cult. Breglia Pulci Doria 1998, 107–108, speaks in the sense of a curotrophic cult, which would have been somehow associated with the demetriac cult of Neapolis.
72 On Athena Ergane, see Consoli 2004, 2010. On textile votive offerings, suggested by loom weights, see Neils 2009. For an analysis of the relationship between crafts and the nuptial education of maidens under the tutelage of Athena, see Portale 2014. This meaning of Athena is also present in the Italic-Roman cult of Minerva, especially in relation to weaving as an element in the preparation of maidens for marriage, see Cinaglia 2017.
73 On these aspects most recently, see Parisi 2017.
74 Poli 2006.
75 Poli 2006, 243; on the same aspect for Pompei, see Parisi 2017, 198.
76 Portale 2012a, 2012b, 2020, 2021 elucidated the significance of protomes with *polos* in Sicelian sanctuaries, also linked to the cult of Athena.
77 See Menichetti 2014, with bibliography. The author emphasises, however, that the ritual in Daunia does not take place in a sanctuary of Athena Ilias. For the

Chronological phases and clues to the nature of the cult 81

connections of the cult of Athena Ilias with rituals of passage, see D'Ercole 1990, 296–298. See also a krater by the Dolone Painter in the Bibliothèque nationale de France, where Athena with a Phrygian helmet (placed on the ground) bathes her hands at a fountain. She is with Hera and Aphrodite: the scene can be interpreted precisely in the sense of a female ritual, for which, see Menichetti 2006.

78 In its widespread diffusion, statuettes of Athena Ilias are found, in the 4th century BC, in the sanctuary of Fondo Patturelli in Capua, clearly linked to a ritual of passage, see Sampaolo 2011, 15.
79 For an overview of the cave's roles in Greece and Magna Graecia, see Mancini 2022, with bibliography. The relationship with nuptial rites is quite important, well pointed out by Lavagne 1988, 67–70, as Pan is dedicated to carnal love in contrast or in opposition to the official love given by marriage: the cave is the usual setting in which such rites can be celebrated. This status is then transferred to the Hellenistic and the Roman cave.
80 On Pan's relationship with the nymphs, see Borgeaud 1988, 155–156; Larson 2001, 96–98.
81 On the role of nymphs in pre-nuptial rituals in the female sphere, see Dalmon 2011.
82 The ritual of bathing in water was also reserved for statues of deities, for which, see Kahil 1994. Callimachus, in the 5th Hymn to Aphrodite, tells of the ritual bathing of the statue of Pallas, for which, see Menichetti 2006.
83 For a summary, see Lippolis 1988–89.
84 Dyggve 1960, 125–126, 445–451.
85 On this subject, see Filser 2022. One could still develop this theme in the relationship between the natural element, or rather the wild, non-manmade landscape, and female rituality, for which, see Cole 2004. See also Ferrari 2003, 2004.
86 Breglia Pulci Doria 1998, 106.
87 Osanna, Giletti 2020.
88 For this meaning of Athena, see Detienne 1970; Giangiulio 1988, 106; Fenet 2016, 21–65 (who also lists Punta Campanella). On the Athena of Punta Campanella in particular, see Breglia Pulci Doria 1995, 39–42, 1998. the latter argues that the goddess of the Sorrento sanctuary is a "marine" and "curotrophic" Athena. A sign of this vocation of the cult would be found in Livy's passage (thunderbolt on the rostral column, hence link to the sea) and that of Statius (ritual for ships passing the strait). Breglia Pulci Doria 2002, 131–132, argues that the "marine" Athena could have been joined by the Athena Ilias at the end of the 4th century BC. However, the contrast proposed by the scholar with "unfavourable divinities" cannot be sustained, given the meaning of the Sirens in the Neapolitan colonial world. See also Cerchiai 2002.
89 On this subject, see Detienne, Vernant 1999.
90 A suggestion on this aspect is offered by Pontrandolfo 2002. D'Alessio 2009, 112, mentions Athena's dual significance as a goddess linked to the female sphere and at the same time, protector of seafarers, already in the archaic period.
91 For the topic, see Fenet 2016, 21–65.
92 Breglia Pulci Doria 1996, 177–178.
93 Rescigno 2010.
94 Rescigno 2010, 194. On the Nocerine League, see Senatore 2001.
95 De Caro 2002 placed this choice in a political key, as part of a Samnite revaluation, under the influence of Rome. Cerchiai 2002 instead emphasises the role of Capua in this sense. D'Alessio 2009, 112, suggests a single political direction, Samnite in character, which directed the three coastal sanctuaries of the Peninsula.

8 Conclusions

In conclusion, the two phases, Archaic in the 6th century BC and the subsequent Classical and late-Classical period, are marked by the presence of a sanctuary whose exact arrangement is currently unknown and can only be hypothesised on the basis of the finds discovered. The architectural, votive and functional materials, however, point towards a sanctuary characterised by extensive interactions between diverse peoples[1], under Greek influence in a territory controlled by the indigenous city of Surrentum.[2] Clearly structured in the Greek fashion, the sanctuary is better described as "frontier" than "extra-urban".[3] It was built by the Euboean cities of Cumae and Neapolis but probably also Posidonia.[4] It hosted the cult of a female divinity, probably Athena, who began to be worshipped in the form of the Trojan variant in the late 5th or 4th century BC, but no later than the second half of the 4th century BC. The development of the sanctuary of Punta Campanella follows the same pattern as the other sanctuaries along the coast[5], especially those of Privati di Stabia and the *Foro Triangolare* in Pompeii.

Following the Archaic and Classical phases, attested by elements of material culture but not by any proper structures, the area of the sanctuary was completely rebuilt: the 2nd century BC saw the construction of the paved road and the portico granting access to the terrace where the cult buildings are believed to have stood. At this time, the entire area acquired functional structures, and the steps leading down to the sea on the west side and the cave on the east side were improved. This was the sanctuary's period of greatest splendour, accounting for the largest quantity of materials so far discovered at the site. As we have seen, the votive coroplastic art, consisting of reproductions of Athena Ilias, *kourotrophoi*, figures linked to fertility and Tanagrines, appears to be in perfect continuity with the previous phase, with the female dimension even more accentuated. From Athena, the cult shifted to Minerva, as is explicit from the Oscan inscription meaningfully located on the steps leading down to the cave on the east side, but this does not seem to have entailed any changes to the elements of the ritual. In addition, the *liber coloniarum* refers to the management of the sanctuary and its territory "occupied by the Greeks", a tangible sign of continuity until the Roman era.

DOI: 10.4324/9781032647548-8

Towards the end of the 2nd century BC, the sanctuaries of Pompeii and Stabiae, which throughout the Hellenistic period developed in parallel with Punta Campanella, seem to have stopped functioning, being either converted to new uses or abandoned.[6] At Punta Campanella, in contrast with what had been previously known, the presence of ceramic material dated to the period from the 1st century BC to the 4th century AD indicates continued occupation of the site, albeit more sporadic than the previous phases, while traces of a Roman villa have not yet been found. The repairs to the paved road and some other structures with reused material seem to indicate a degree of refurbishment aimed at prolonging the life of the sanctuary, which by then, however, was used only occasionally, having begun a steady and inexorable decline.

Notes

1 On mediterranean sanctuaries, see recently Russo Tagliente, Guarnieri 2016.
2 Guzzo 1992, 155, writes of a sanctuary connected with the indigenous city of Sorrento. Russo 1992 speaks of a frontier sanctuary of possible Etruscan-Italic origin on the basis of the material found. Breglia Pulci Doria 1995 argues the Etruscan origin of Sorrento, while the Athenaion would be "Greek". D'Alessio 2009, 111, speaks of the "indigenous" Punta Campanella.
3 The sanctuary is a long way from Cumae and Neapolis, but divides, as we have seen, the two gulfs under the influence of Cumae/Neapolis and Posidonia. On extra-urban and frontier sanctuaries the bibliography is vast. For those that can be defined as frontier, see Guzzo 1987 and *Atti Taranto* 1999, in particular Osanna 1999. On extra-urban sanctuaries, see Asheri 1988; Leone 1998; de Polignac 1999. See the recent synthesis by Greco 2021b.
4 Mele 2016, 289 is rightly of this opinion, also based on the architectural materials identified by Rescigno 2010, 185–186.
5 Also around Castro, cults of Athena Ilias developed at some point along the coast of Salento, see D'Andria 2020, 131–132.
6 For a summary: D'Alessio 2001, 173–174, 2009, 113.

Bibliography

Journal abbreviations follow the Archäologische Bibliographie of the Deutsches Archäologisches Institut.

Adinolfi, G., Senatore, F. 2015. "*Promunturium Minervae* (in margine a una nuova interpretazione di esskazsiúm in RIX ST CM 2 e ai recenti restauri di Via Campanella)", *Oebalus* 10: 275–370.

Albore Livadie, C. (a cura di). 1990. "La Penisola Sorrentina nella Preistoria e nella Protostoria", in *Archeologia a Piano di Sorrento: Ricerche di preistoria e di protostoria nella Peninsula Sorrentina*, Catalogo della mostra (Piano di Sorrento, 7 dicembre 1990–20 gennaio 1991), Napoli: 23–37.

———. 1992. "Cenni preliminari sugli scavi in loc. Trinità (Piano di Sorrento, 1987–1990)", *AIONArch* 14: 221–237.

———. 2001. "La necropoli arcaica di via Madonna delle Grazie (Comuni di Santa Maria la Carità e di Gragnano)", in Bonifacio, G., Sodo, A.M., Ascione, G.C. (eds.), *In Stabiano. Cultura e archeologia da Stabiae: La città e il territorio tra l'età arcaica e l'età romana*, Catalogo della mostra (Castellammare di Stabia, 4 novembre 2000–31 gennaio 2001), Castellammare di Stabia: 17–18.

———. 2010. "La Campania media e la Penisola sorrentino-amalfitana dall'età del Rame all'età del Ferro: Alcune situazioni a confronto", in Senatore, Russo 2010: 149–175.

Anastasio, F. 1732. *Lucubrationes in Surrentinorum Ecclesiasticas Civilesque Antiquitates nuncupatae Sanctissimo Domino Nostro Clementi XII Pont. Max. a Philippo Anastasio Patriarcha Antiocheno pridem Archiepiscopo Surrentino. Pars altera*, Romae.

Anastasio, L.A. 1751. *Animadversiones in librum F. Pii Thomae Milante Episcopi Stabiensi de Stabiis*, Neapoli.

Andò, V. 1996. "*Nymphe*: La sposa e le Ninfe", *QuadUrbin* 52, no. 1: 47–79.

Asheri, D. 1988. "À propos des sanctuaries extra – urbains en Sicilie et Grande – Grèce: Théories et témoignages", in *Mélanges P. Lévêque*, I, Paris: 1–15.

Athenaion. 2023. D'Andria, F., Degl'Innocenti, E., Caggia, M.P., Ismaelli, T., Mancini, L. (a cura di), Athenaion. *Tarantini, Messapi e altri nel santuario di Atena a Castro*, Catalogo della mostra (Taranto-Castro, 2022–2023), Bari.

Atti Taranto. 1999. *Conini e frontiera nella grecità d'Occidente*, Atti del XXXVII Convegno di Studi sulla Magna Grecia (Taranto, 3–6 ottobre 1997), Taranto.

Battiloro, I., Mogetta, M. 2021. "Il Santuario di Venere. Scavi 2017–2019", in M. Osanna (a cura di), *Ricerche e scoperte a Pompei: In ricordo di Enzo Lippolis*, Roma: 35–56.

Beloch, K.J. 1989. *Campania: Storia e topografia della Napoli antica e dei suoi contorni*, Napoli (re-edited by G. Pugliese Carratelli).

Bonghi Jovino, M. 1982. *La necropoli preromana di Vico Equense*, Cava dei Tirreni.

———. 2008. *Mitici approdi e paesaggi culturali: La Penisola Sorrentina prima di Roma*, Castellammare di Stabia.

Borgeaud, P. 1988. *The cult of Pan in ancient Greece*, Chicago.

Braccesi, L. 2010. *Sulle rotte di Ulisse: L'invenzione della geografia omerica*, Bari.

Breglia Pulci Doria, L. 1987. "Le Sirene, il canto, la morte, la *polis*", *AIONarch* 9: 65–99.

———. 1990. "Le Sirene, il confine, l'aldilà", in Mactoux, M.-M., Geny, E. (éds.), *Mélanges Pierre Lévéque*, Paris: 63–78.

———. 1992. "Athena e le Sirene?" in *Campanella* 1992: 179–182.

———. 1995. "Il mare, il paesaggio, la rotta: Osservazioni sui culti greci in penisola sorrentina", *La Terra delle Sirene* 12: 21–42.

———. 1996. "Sorrento: La documentazione letteraria", in *Dalla Magna Grecia a Cos: Ricerche di storia antica*, Napoli: 157–187.

———. 1998. "Atena e il mare: Appunti *sull'Athenaion* di Punta della Campanella", in *I culti della Campania antica* 1998: 97–108.

———. 2002. "Elmo frigio, Atena Ilias, Palladio", in *Elmo frigio* 2002: 103–136.

Breglia, L. 2016. "Le Sirene: Un'identità sorrentina?" in Pepe, C., Rescigno, C., Senatore, F. (a cura di), *Sirene*, Atti del VI ciclo di conferenze (Piano di Sorrento, 2013), Roma: 1–14.

Budetta, T. 1996. "Sorrento, Massa Lubrense. Località il Vadabilo. La necropoli tardoarcaica del Deserto di Sant'Agata sui due Golfi", *BA* 39–40: 135–138.

———. 1999. *Il Museo Archeologico Territoriale della Penisola Sorrentina "Georges Vallet"*, Bracigliano.

———. 2001. *Vico Equense, l'antiquarium: Storia di una raccolta*, Napoli.

Budetta, T., Cannavacciuolo, R., Rizzo, C. 2018. "*Via Minervia*: Nuovi dati dalle recenti indagini a Punta della Campanella", in *The archaeology of death*, Proceedings of the Seventh Conference of Italian Archaeology (National University of Ireland, Galway, 16–18 April 2016), Oxford: 365–370.

Campanella. 1992. *Il santuario di Punta della Campanella*, Atti della Giornata di Studio (Napoli, 16 dicembre 1991), (in *AIONarch* 14, 1992), Napoli.

Capasso, B. 1846. *Topografia storico-archeologica della penisola sorrentina e raccolta di antiche iscrizioni edite ed inedite appartenenti alla medesima*, Napoli.

Caputo, M.T. 2004. "Il promontorio di Minerva: Nuove conquiste topografiche", in Senatore, F. (a cura di), *Pompei, Capri e la Penisola Sorrentina*, Atti del quinto ciclo di conferenze di conferenze di geologia, storia e archeologia (Pompei, Anacapri, Scafati, Castellamare di Stabia, ottobre 2002 – aprile 2003), Capri: 51–101.

Carafa, P. 2008. *Culti e santuari della Campania antica*, Roma.

Cascella, S. 2017. "Scavi lungo il tracciato dell'Appia e i suoi diverticoli a sud di Sinuessa: Dati preliminari", *Oebalus* 12: 7–77.

Cerchiai, L. 2002. "Il tipo dell'Atena Frigia in area campana", *Elmo Frigio* 2002: 29–36.

———. 2017. "Brevi riflessioni sulle Sirene di Sorrento", in Greco, G., Ferrara, B., Cicala, L. (a cura di), *Kithon Lydios. Studi di storia e archeologia con Giovanna Greco*, Napoli: 61–65.

Cinaglia, T. 2017. "Minerva ed i *pueri*: Proposta per una rilettura di alcune fonti letterarie", *Gerión* 35, no. 1: 77–100.

Bibliography

Cipriani, M. 2002. "L'immagine di Athena negli ex-voto del santuario settentrionale di Paestum", *Elmo Frigio* 2002: 37–46.

Cipriani, M., Avagliano, G. 2005. "Materiali votivi dall'*Athenaion* di Paestum", in Comella, A., Mele, S. (a cura di), *Depositi votivi e culti dell'Italia antica dall'età arcaica a quella tardo-repubblicana*, Atti del Convegno di Studi (Perugia, 1–4 giugno 2000), Bari: 555–667.

Cole, S.G. 2004. *Landscapes, gender, and ritual space*, Berkeley-Los Angeles-London.

Consoli, V. 2004. "Atena Ergane. Sorgere di un culto sull'Acropoli di Atene", *ASAtene* 82: 31–60.

———. 2010. "Elmo, fuso e conocchia: Per un'iconografia di Atena Ergane", *Eidola* 7: 9–28.

Cruccas, E. 2007. "Παρθένοι e σφαιρίσεις: Alcune considerazioni sul rituale delle *arrephoroi* attraverso l'analisi di un frammento di *hydria* conservato al Museum Schloß Hohentübingen", *Siris* 8: 5–20.

Culti della Campania antica. 1998. Adamo Muscettola, S., Greco, G. (a cura di), *I culti della Campania antica*, Atti del convegno internazionale di studi in ricordo di Nazarena Valenza Mele (Napoli, 15–17 maggio 1995), Napoli.

d'Agostino, B. 1992. "Dov'era il santuario delle Sirene?" in *Campanella* 1992: 171–172.

D'Alessio, M.T. 2001. *Materiali votivi dal Foro Triangolare di Pompei*, Roma.

———. 2009. *I culti a Pompei: Divinità, luoghi e frequentatori*, Roma.

———. 2011. "Spazio, funzioni e paesaggio nei santuari a terrazze italici di età tardo-repubblicana. Note per un approccio sistemico al linguaggio di una grande architettura", in La Rocca, E., D'Alessio, A. (a cura di), *Tradizione e innovazione: L'elaborazione del linguaggio ellenistico nell'architettura romana e italica di età tardo-repubblicana*, Roma: 51–86.

Dalmon, S. 2011. "Les Nymphes dans les rites du marriage", *Cahiers "Mondes anciens"* 2: 1–16 (http://journals.openedition.org/mondesanciens/400).

D'Ambrosio, A. 1984. *La stipe votiva in località Bottaro (Pompei)*, Napoli.

D'Andria, F. 2020. "*L'Athenaion* di Castro in Messapia", *RM* 126: 79–140.

De Angelis d'Ossat, G. 1977. "L'architettura delle "terme" di Baia", in *I Campi Flegrei nell'archeologia e nella storia*, Atti del Convegno Internazionale (Roma, 4–7 maggio 1976), Roma: 227–274.

De Caro, S. 1992. "Appunti sull'Atena della Punta della Campanella", in *Campanella* 1992: 173–178.

D'Ercole, M.C. 1990. *La stipe votiva del Belvedere a Lucera*, Roma.

de Polignac, F. 1999. "L'installation des dieux et la genèse des cités en Grèce d'Occident, une question résolue? Rétour à Mégara Hyblaea", in *La colonisation grecque en Méditerranée occidentale*, Actes de la rencontre scientiique (Rome-Naples, 15–18 novembre 1995), Paris: 209–229.

De Simone, A., Borriello, M.R. 1985. "La stipe di S. Aniello", in Pozzi, E. (a cura di), *Napoli antica*, Catalogo della mostra (Napoli, 26 settembre 1985–15 aprile 1986), Napoli: 159–170.

Detienne, M. 1970. "Le navire d'Athéna", *RHistRel* 178: 133–177.

Detienne, M., Vernant, J.P. 1999. *Le astuzie dell'intelligenza nella Grecia antica*, Roma-Bari 1999.

de Waele, J.A.K.E. 2001. *Il tempio dorico del Foro triangolare di Pompei*, Roma.

Di Franco, L., Laudonia, T. 2022. "La città di *Surrentum* tra medio impero e tardo-antico: Dall'impianto urbano alla fase di rifunzionalizzazione e abbandono della villa di Agrippa Postumo", in Cimadomo, P., Nappo, D. (a cura di), *A global crisis? The Mediterranean world between the 3rd and the 5th century CE*, Rome: 179–223.

Di Luca, G. 2009. "*Nullus in orbe sinus Bais praelucet amoenis*: Riflessioni sull'architettura dei complessi c.d. 'dell'Ambulatio', 'della Sosandra' e delle 'Piccole Terme' a Baia", *BABesch* 84: 143–162.

Doni agli dei. 2008. Greco, G., Ferrara, B. (a cura di), *Doni agli dei. Il sistema dei doni votivi nei santuari*, Pozzuoli.

Dyggve, E. 1960. *Lindos: Fouilles de l'acropole, 1902–1914 et 1952, 3. Le sanctuaire d'Athana Lindia et l'architecture lindienne*, Berlin-Copenaghen.

Elmo frigio. 2002. Cerchiai, L. (a cura di), *L'iconografia di Atena con elmo frigio in Italia meridionale*, Atti della giornata di studi (Fisciano, 12 giugno 1998), Napoli.

Federico, E. 1998. "Capri dall'espansione cumana nel Golfo (VII a.C.) al foedus Neapolitanum (326 a.C.)", in Federico, E., Miranda, E. (a cura di), *Capri antica. Dalla preistoria alla fine dell'età romana*, Capri: 375–415.

———. 2010a. "*Seirenoussai* o *Seirenes*. Una semplice nuance? Strabone, le Sirene, Li Galli", in Senatore, Russo 2010: 255–289.

———. 2010b. "Le Sirene, la morte e il destino di pietra. Impressioni mitiche nel paesaggio naturale", in Aragona, R. (a cura di), *Illusione e seduzione*, Napoli: 97–101.

Fenet, A. 2016. *Les dieux olympiens et la mer: Espaces et pratiques cultuelles*, Rome.

Ferrara, B. 2009. *I pozzi votivi nel santuario di Hera alla foce del Sele*, Pozzuoli.

Ferrari, G. 2003. "What kind of rite of passage was the ancient Greek wedding?" in Dodd, D.B., Faraone, C.A. (eds.), *Initiation in ancient Greek rituals and narratives: New critical perspectives*, London-New York: 27–42.

———. 2004. "The 'Anodos' of the bride", in Yatromanolakis, D., Roilos, P. (eds.), *Greek ritual poetics*, Washington-Athens: 246–260.

Fiammenghi, C.A. 1985. "Agropoli. Primi saggi di scavo nell'area del Castello", *AIONarch* 7: 53–68.

Filser, W., Fritsch, B., Kennedy, W., Klose, C., Perrella, M.R. 2017. "Surrounded by the sea: Re-investigating the villa maritima del Capo di Sorrento. Interim report", *JRA* 30: 65–95.

———. 2022. "Vari, Lindo, Praeneste e Platone: Sulla genesi della grotta d'arte grecoromana", in Di Franco, L., Perrella, R. (a cura di), *Le grotte tra Preistoria, età classica e Medioevo: Capri, la Campania, il Mediterraneo*, Atti del Convegno Internazionale di Studi (Capri-Anacapri, 7–9 ottobre 2021), Roma: 345–366.

Giampaola, D., Greco, E. 2022. *Napoli prima di Napoli: Mito e fondazioni della città di Partenope*, Roma.

Giangiulio, M. 1986. "Appunti di storia dei culti", in *Neapolis*, Atti del XXV Convegno di Studi sulla Magna Grecia (Taranto, 3–7 ottobre 1985), Taranto: 101–154.

———. 1988. "Tra mare e terra: L'orizzonte religioso del paesaggio costiero", in Prontera, F. (a cura di), *La Magna Grecia e il mare: Studi di storia marittima*, Taranto: 251–271.

Giannettasio, N.P. 1696. *Aestates surrentinae*, Neapoli.

———. 1722. *Autumni Surrentini*, Neapoli.

Giuliani, C.F. 1973. "Contributi allo studio della tipologia dei criptoportici", in Etienne R. (ed.), *Les cryptoportiques dans l'architecture romaine*, Rome: 79–115.

Gras, M. 1993. "Pour une Méditerranée des *emporia*", in Bresson, A., Rouillard, P. (éds.), *L'emporion*, Paris: 103–112.

Greco, E. 1992. "Nel Golfo di Napoli: Tra Sirene, Sirenusse e Athena", in *Campanella* 1992: 161–170.

———. 1995. "Strabone e la Penisola Sorrentina", *La Terra delle Sirene* 11: 9–15.
Greco, G. 2017. "Il golfo cumano e Siracusa: Incontri di uomini e culture", in Panvini R. (a cura di), *Migrazioni e commerci in Sicilia, modelli del passato come paradigma del presente*, Palermo: 157–184.
———. 2021a. "La terra di Athena nel golfo cumano: Un tassello mancante nella costruzione di una leggenda", in de Fidio, P., Gigante Lanzara, V., Rigo, A. (a cura di), *Scritti in memoria di Giovanni Pugliese Carratelli*, II (= *PP* 76, no. 1–2), Firenze: 91–116.
———. 2021b. "Achei di Occidente e santuari extraurbani: Per un riesame dei dati", in Ployer, R., Svoboda-Baas, D. (Hrsg.), Magnis Itineribus. *Festschrift für Verena Gassner zum 65. Geburtstag*, Wien: 65–70.
Guzzo, P.G. 1987. "Schema per la categoria interpretativa del 'santuario di frontiera'", *ScAnt* 1: 373–379.
———. 1992. "Introduzione", in *Campanella* 1992: 151–160.
———. 2016. *Le città di Magna Grecia e di Sicilia dal VI al I secolo, I. La Magna Grecia*, Roma.
Håland, E.J. 2012. "The ritual year of Athena: The agricultural cycle of the olive, girls' rites of passage, and official ideology", *Journal of Religious History* 36, no. 2: 256–284.
Jacobelli, L. 1994. "Alcune osservazioni sull'area di Punta Campanella", in Capasso, M., Puglia, E. (a cura di), *Scritti di varia umanità in memoria di Benito Iezzi*, Sorrento: 65–77.
Kahil, L. 1994. "Bains de statues et de divinité", in Ginouvès, R., Guimier-Sorbets, A.-M., Jouanna, J. (éds.), *L'eau, la santé et la maladie dans le monde grec*, Actes du colloque organisé à Paris (CNRS et Fondation Singer-Polignac) du 25 au 27 novembre 1992 par le Centre de recherche "Archéologie et systèmes d'information" et par l'URA 1255 "Médecine grecque", Athènes-Paris: 217–223.
Larson, J. 2001. *Greek nymphs: Myth, cult, lore*, Oxford.
Laubscher, H.P. 1980. "Ein Athenakopf im Museo Barracco", in Simon, E. (Hrsg.), *Tainia: Roland Hampe zum 70. Geburtstag am 2. Dezember 1978*, Mainz: 227–237.
Laudonia, T. 2013. "Materiali dalle necropoli preromane della Penisola Sorrentina nelle collezioni del Museo Correale di Terranova: Alcune note preliminari", *Oebalus* 8: 301–323.
Lavagne, H. 1988. *Operosa Antra: Recherches sur la grotte à Rome de Sylla à Hadrien*, Rome.
Leone, R. 1998. *Luoghi di culto extraurbani d'età arcaica in Magna Grecia*, Torino.
Lippolis, E. 1988–89. "Il santuario di Athana a Lindo", *ASAtene* 66: 97–157.
Maddoli, G. 1991. "I culti della Campania antica. I culti greci", in *Storia e civiltà della Campania. L'Evo antico*, Napoli: 247–270.
Mancini, L. 2007. "Sirene e civette: Il 'bestiario alato' di Atena", *Oebalus* 2: 49–79.
Mancini, Loren. 2020. "Taranto e l'affermazione del linguaggio ellenistico in Messapia. Considerazioni sull'architettura funeraria e gli spazi del sacro", in Degl'Innocenti, E. (a cura di), *Il tesoretto di Specchia al Museo Archeologico Nazionale di Taranto. Taranto e la Messapia tra IV e III sec. a.C.*, Foggia: 41–65.
———. 2022. "L'Antro delle Ninfe. Le grotte come luoghi ierofanici tra Grecia e Magna Grecia", in Di Franco, L., Perrella, R. (a cura di), *Le grotte tra Preistoria, età classica e Medioevo: Capri, la Campania, il Mediterraneo*, Atti del Convegno Internazionale di Studi (Capri-Anacapri, 7–9 ottobre 2021), Roma: 289–320.

Maurizi, N. 1993–95. "La presenza ateniese a Napoli: Aspetti mitici, culti, tradizione storica", *AnnPerugia* 31: 287–309.

Mele, A. 2007. "Atene e la Magna Grecia", in Greco, E., Lombardo, M. (a cura di), *Atene e l'Occidente. I grandi temi*, Atti del Convegno Internazionale (Atene, 25–27 maggio 2006), Atene: 239–268.

———. 2009. "Tra subcolonia ed *epoikia:* Il caso di *Neapolis*", in Lombardo, M., Frisone, F. (a cura di), *Colonie di colonie: Le fondazioni sub-coloniali greche tra colonizzazione e colonialismo*, Atti del Convegno (Lecce, 22–24 giugno 2006), Galatina: 183–201.

———. 2014. *Greci in Campania*, Roma.

———. 2016. "Le Sirene nel Tirreno", *Oebalus* 11: 259–324.

Menichetti, M. 2006. "Lo specchio di Hera e gli 'specchi' di Atena su un vaso del Pittore di Dolone", in Massa-Pairault, F.H. (éd.), *L'image antique et son interprétation*, Rome: 261–275.

———. 2014. "Cassandra e le altre fanciulle. Miti e riti", *Aitia* 4 (http://journals.open edition.org/aitia/1016).

Mingazzini, P., Pfister, F. 1946. *Forma Italiae, Regio I, Latium et Campania. II, Surrentum*, Firenze.

Miniero, P. 2002. "Il deposito votivo in località Privati presso Castellammare di Stabia: Nota preliminare", *Elmo Frigio* 2002: 11–27.

———. 2005. "Deposito votivo in località Privati presso Castellammare di Stabia (NA)", in Comella, A., Mele, S. (a cura di), *Depositi votivi e culti dell'Italia antica dall'età arcaica a quella tardo-repubblicana*, Atti del Convegno di Studi (Perugia, 1–4 giugno 2000), Bari: 525–534.

Miniero, P., D'Ambrosio, A., Sodo, A., Bonifacio, G., Di Giovanni, V., Cantilena, R. 1997. "Il santuario in località Privati presso Castellammare di Stabia: Osservazioni preliminari", *RStPomp* 8: 11–56.

Morel, J.P. 1982. "Marina di Ieranto, Punta della Campanella: Observations archéologiques dans la presqu'île de Sorrente", in Ἀπαρχαί. *Nuove ricerche e studi sulla Magna Grecia e la Sicilia antica in onore di P. E. Arias*, Pisa: 147–153.

Mugione, E. 2002. "Le immagini di Atena con elmo frigio nella ceramica italiota", *Elmo Frigio*: 63–80.

Neils, J. 2009. "Textile dedications to female deities: The case of the peplos", in Prêtre, C., Huysecom-Haxhi, S. (éds.), *Le donateur, l'offrande et la déesse: Systèmes votifs dans les sanctuaires de déesses du monde grec*, Actes du 31e colloque international organisé par l'UMR HALMA-IPEL (Université Charles-de-Gaulle, Lille, 13–15 décembre 2007), Liège: 149–167.

Osanna, M. 1999. "Territorio coloniale e frontiera: La documentazione archeologica", in *Atti Taranto* 1999: 273–292.

———. 2017. "Nuove ricerche nei santuari pompeiani", in Lippolis, E., Osanna, M. (a cura di), *I Pompeiani e i loro dei. Culti, rituali e funzioni sociali a Pompei*, Atti della Giornata di Studi (Roma, 15 Febbraio 2016) (= *ScAnt* 22.3, 2016), Roma: 71–88.

Osanna, M., Gerogiannis, G., Giletti, F. 2021. "Nuovi scavi dall'area del Foro Triangolare di Pompei: Note preliminari", in Osanna, M. (a cura di), *Ricerche e scoperte a Pompei: In ricordo di Enzo Lippolis*, Roma: 17–34.

Osanna, M., Giletti, F. 2020. "Il Foro Triangolare di Pompei tra vecchie acquisizioni e nuovi scavi", *RStPomp* 31: 7–24.

Osanna, M., Rescigno, C. 2021. "Pompei, Sorrento e la battaglia di Cuma", *RendLinc* 32, no. 1–2: 199–226.

Pais, E. 1908. "Il culto di Atena Siciliana e l'*Athenaion* della Punta della Campanella", in *Ricerche storiche e geografiche sull'Italia antica*, Torino: 275–294.

Pappalardo, U. 1993. "Iezzi e le 'Passeggiate sorrentine' di Amedeo Maiuri", *La Terra delle Sirene* 7: 63–70.

Parisi, V. 2017. "Le terrecotte figurate e l'uso rituale dei *signa fictilia* nelle aree sacre pubbliche della Pompei preromana. Elementi per una sintesi", in Lippolis, E., Osanna, M., Lepone, A. (a cura di), *I Pompeiani e i loro dei. Culti, rituali e funzioni sociali a Pompei*, Atti della Giornata di Studi (Roma, 15 febbraio 2016) (= *ScAnt* 22.3, 2016), Roma: 185–205.

Poccetti, P. 2010. "Intorno ai nuovi documenti di area sorrentina: Riflessioni sul *novum* e sul *notum*", in Senatore, Russo 2010: 65–101.

———. 2016. "Il nome di Sorrento e le Sirene", *Oebalus* 11: 326–373.

Poli, N. 2006. "Vasellame miniaturistico dell'Italia meridionale", *QuadFriulA* 16: 239–246.

Pollone, S., Romano, L. 2015. "Transformations and permanence's of landscape and architecture: The Minerva Tower of Punta Campanella in the Sorrento-Amalfi Peninsula", in Rodríguez-Navarro, P. (ed.), *Defensive architecture of the Mediterranean. XV to XVIII centuries*, II, Proceedings of the International Conference on Modern Age Fortifications of the Western Mediterranean Coast FORTMED 2015, Valencia: 273–280.

Pontrandolfo, A. 2002. "Atena frigia: Un'immagine polisemica", *Elmo Frigio* 2002: 147–152.

Portale, E.C. 2012a. "Busti fittili e Ninfe: Sulla valenza e la polisemia delle rappresentazioni abbreviate in forma di busto nella coroplastica votiva siceliota", in Albertocchi, M., Pautasso, A. (a cura di), *Philotechnia: Studi sulla coroplastica della Sicilia greca*, Napoli: 227–253.

———. 2012b. "Le *nymphai* e l'acqua in Sicilia: Contesti rituali e morfologia dei votivi", in Calderone, A. (a cura di), *Cultura e religione delle acque*, Roma: 169–191.

———. 2014. "Le opere di Atena: Identità femminile e *philergia* nella Sicilia greca", in Caminneci, V. (a cura di), *Le opere e i giorni: Lavoro, produzione e commercio tra passato e presente*, Atti e contributi del corso di formazione per docenti (Progetto Scuola-Museo 2012–2013), Palermo: 63–104.

———. 2020. "Iconografia votiva e performances rituali: Qualche esempio dalla Sicilia greca", in Caruso, F., Gigli, R. (a cura di), *Sikelika Hiera. Approcci multidisciplinari allo studio del sacro nella Sicilia greca*, Atti del Convegno (Catania, 11–12 giugno 2010), Catania: 111–124.

———. 2021. "Rappresentazioni del sacro femminile. I busti femminili 'di tipo agrigentino' in contesto", in Bonanno, D., Buttitta, I.E. (a cura di), *Narrazioni e rappresentazioni del sacro femminile*, Atti del convegno internazionale di studi in memoria di Giuseppe Martorana, Palermo: 165–203.

Prontera, F. 2003. *Tabula Peutingeriana: Le antiche vie del mondo*, Firenze.

Puglia, E. 1995. "Marmi antichi della Campanella nel convento sorrentino di S. Vincenzo", *La Terra delle Sirene* 11: 17–21.

———. 2016. "L'anfora lubrense con la sirena del Museo 'G. Vallet'", in Pepe, C., Rescigno, C., Senatore F. (a cura di), *Sirene*, Atti del VI ciclo di conferenze (Piano di Sorrento, 2013), Roma: 15–28.

Bibliography 91

Pugliese Carratelli, G. 1990. "Commento storico", in Russo 1990: 275–278.
Quilici, L. 2002. "La via Appia. Iniziative e interventi per la conoscenza e la valorizzazione da Roma a Capua", *Atlante Tematico di Topografia Antica* 11: 107–146.
———. 2004. "Santuari, ville e mausolei sul percorso della Via Appia al valico degli Aurunci", *Atlante Tematico di Topografia Antica* 13: 441–542.
Rescigno, C. 1998. "Tetti campani di età classica", in *I culti della Campania antica*, Atti del Convegno Internazionale di Studi in ricordo di Nazarena Valenza Mele (Napoli, 15–17 maggio 1995), Roma: 129–141.
———. 2010. "Note sulla forma urbana di *Surrentum*", in Senatore, Russo 2010: 177–200.
———. 2016. "Stili architettonici occidentali tra identità politica e distretti culturali", in Polis e Politeiai *nella Magna Grecia arcaica e classica*, Atti del LIII Convegno di Studi sulla Magna Grecia (Taranto, 26–29 settembre 2013), Taranto: 459–474.
Rescigno, C., Senatore, F. 2009. "Le città della piana campana tra IV e III sec. a.C.: Dati storici e topografici", in Osanna, M. (a cura di), *Verso la città. Forme insediative in Lucania e nel mondo italico tra IV e III sec. a.C.*, Venosa: 415–462.
Rispoli, M. 2013. "Una tomba a ricettacolo dalla necropoli di Trinità a Piano di Sorrento", *Oebalus* 8: 121–145.
Russo, M. 1990. *Punta della Campanella: Epigrafe rupestre osca e reperti vari dall'Athenaion*, Roma.
———. 1992. "Materiali arcaici e tardo-arcaici dalla stipe *dell'Athenaion* di Punta della Campanella", in *Campanella* 1992: 201–219.
———. 1997. *Sorrento: Archeologia tra l'Hotel Vittoria e Capo Circe. Scavi e rinvenimenti dal Settecento a oggi*, Sorrento.
———. 1998. "Il territorio tra Stabia e Punta della Campanella nell'antichità", in Senatore, F. (a cura di), *Pompei, il Sarno e la Penisola Sorrentina*, Atti del primo ciclo di conferenze di geologia, storia e archeologia (Pompei, Aprile-Giugno 1997), Pompei: 23–98.
———. 1999. "Sorrento: Edifici pubblici, case private e *tabernae* tra età ellenistica e tardo-antico lungo due assi viari", in Senatore, F. (a cura di), *Pompei, il Vesuvio e la penisola Sorrentina*, Atti del secondo ciclo di conferenze di geologia, storia e archeologia (Pompei, ottobre 1997–febbraio 1998), Roma: 145–231.
Russo Tagliente, A., Guarneri, F. (a cura di). 2016. *Santuari mediterranei tra Oriente e Occidente: Interazioni e contatti culturali*, Atti del Convegno Internazionale (Civitavecchia-Roma 2014), Roma.
Salomies, O. 2012. "The *nomina* of Samnites: A checklist", *Arctos* 46: 137–185.
Sampaolo, V. 1984. "Massalubrense (Napoli)", *StEtr* 52: 505–506.
———. 1990. "La Penisola Sorrentina in età arcaica e classica", in Albore Livadie 1990: 109–118.
———. 1992a. "Aspetti culturali della Penisola Sorrentina", in Cristofani, M., Zevi, F. (a cura di), *Omaggio a Paola Zancani Montuoro*, Atti del Convegno organizzato dall'Università di Napoli Federico II (Napoli, 2–5 dicembre 1989), Roma: 99–109.
———. 1992b. "La presenza della Soprintendenza Archeologica a Massa Lubrense", in *I beni culturali di Massa Lubrense, contributo alla conoscenza*, Castellammare di Stabia: 133–140.
———. 2011. "I nuovi scavi del fondo Patturelli. Elementi per una definizione topografica", *Acme* 64, no. 2: 7–20.
Savarese, A. 1963. "Vico Equense Romana", *NapNobil* 3, no. 4: 148–153.

Scatozza Höricht, L. 1997. "Le terrecotte architettoniche del Tempio Dorico di Pompei. L'eredità arcaica", in Lulof, P.S., Moormann, E.M. (eds.), *Deliciae fictiles II*, Proceedings of the Second International Conference on Archaic Architectural Terracottas from Italy (Rome, 12–13 June 1996), Amsterdam: 189–197.

Senatore, F. 2001. "La lega nucerina", in Senatore, F. (a cura di), *Pompei tra Sorrento e Sarno*, Atti del terzo e quarto ciclo di conferenze di geologia, storia e archeologia (Pompei, gennaio 1999 – maggio 2000), Roma: 185–265.

———. 2014. "Le Sirene, il mito e la Penisola Sorrentina", in Adinolfi, G., Senatore, F., *L'incanto delle Sirene*, Napoli: 3–87.

———. 2020. "Le *Seirenoussai* tra i Golfi di Cuma e Posidonia", *Oebalus* 15: 169–236.

Senatore, F., Russo, M. (a cura di). 2010. *Sorrento e la Penisola Sorrentina tra Italici, Etruschi e Greci nel contesto della Campania antica*, Atti della giornata di studi in omaggio a Paola Zancani Montuoro (1901–1987) (Sorrento, 19 maggio 2007), Roma.

Sorrentino, R., Viscione, M. 2001. "Località Madonna delle Grazie. La necropoli classica ed ellenistica", in Bonifacio, G., Sodo, A.M., Ascione, G.C. (a cura di), In Stabiano. *Cultura e archeologia da Stabiae: La città e il territorio tra l'età arcaica e l'età romana*, Catalogo della mostra (Castellammare di Stabia, 4 novembre 2000–31 gennaio 2001), Castellammare di Stabia: 19–20.

Torelli, M. 2002. "Un primo bilancio", *Elmo Frigio* 2002: 137–144.

Triantafillis, E. 2014. "Sull'iscrizione di Punta della Campanella *(Rix, St Cm 2)*: Sannita esskazstum tra ermeneutica e morfologia", *StEtr* 77: 392–402.

von Mercklin, E. 1962. *Antike Figuralkapitelle*, Berlin.

Wolf, M. 2009. "Forschungen zur Tempelarchitektur Pompejis. Der Venus-Tempel im Rahmen des pompejanischen Tempelbaus", *RM* 115: 221–335.

Zancani Montuoro, P. 1983. "Resti di tombe di VI sec. a.C. presso Sorrento", *RendLinc* 38: 143–150.

———. 1987. "Resti di tombe di VI sec. a.C. presso Sorrento", *RendLinc* 42: 7–10.

———. 1990. "Riepilogo sui rinvenimenti e sul culto del santuario", in Russo 1990: 257–260.

Index

Note: Page numbers in *italics* indicate a figure. Page numbers followed by "n" with numbers refer to notes.

Aestates surrentinae 6
Anastasio, F. 6
Anastasio, L.A. 6
ancient road, in Punta Campanella 13, 27; assays *31–32*; composition of 30; current state of road and reconstruction *29*; dry-stone retaining walls *28*, *29*; in Fossa di Papa district 30; interlocking blocks *28*; terracing of *29*; walls in *opus incertum* 27, 30
Aphrodite 65, 70, 80n70, 81n77, n82
approdo di levante (Eastern Landing) 6, 44, 51, 55, 59
approdo di ponente (Western Landing) 52
archaeological investigations, at Punta Campanella; in 1966 8; in 1968 and 1978 8; between 1977 and 1979 9; between 1979 and 1984 9–10; in 1990 13; in 2003 13; in 2004 13; in 2015 and 2016 13
archaelogical site; plan in ancient Via Minervia *14*; of Punta Campanella 1; the road 52; on Sorrentine Peninsula 20–21, *53*, *60*; structures 52; terraces 52
archaeological storage, in Massa Lubrense; Athena Ilias heads *69*; Hellenistic head *70*; *kourotrophos* figurines *69*; late archaic heads *67*; polos, female head with *71*; statuette of Athena Ilias *68*; votive cups *75*
archaic heads *67*

arrephorae (Athenian festival) 80n70
Athena Ilias *68*, *69*, 73, 76, 77n29, 79n49, 79n60, 80n68, 80–81n77, 81n88, 82
Athena 6, 64–66, *68*, *69*, 78n49, 79n60; characteristics of 74; cults of 73–74, 79n60; eighth and seventh centuries BC 73; fifth century BC 73–74; in Lindos 75; late fourth century BC 73, 74; meaning of 81n88; of Punta Campanella 81n88; Phrygian 78–79n49; sanctuary of 52, 71; Sirens and 76n3, 77n19; sixth century BC 73, 79n50; Trojan 78–79n49; of Troy 74, 78n49
athenaion acroterion (Cape Athenaeum) 3
Ausonian population 17

Bay of Ieranto (Baia di Ieranto) 8, 27, 64, 75
Beloch, K.J. 7, 52, 64
Breglia Pulci Doria, L. 64–65, 77n19, 78n42, n43

Cala di Mitigliano 27
Cancello districts 13, 27, 30, 59
Capri 1, 8, 18, 52, 64
caves 57, 58, 61, 82; roles in Greece 75, 81n79; roles in Magna Graecia 81n79
ceramic: achromatic 23; classes 10; figured 65; fragments/discards 8, 25; Ionic tradition 13;

Coppola, A. 10
Cumae 17, 71; colonists from 65; battle of 21; role in cult of Sirens 77n20, 78n42–n44, 82, 83n3

d'Agostino, B. 64
D'Andria, F. 73
Diodorus Siculus 3
Diotimos 73, 78n46

Eastern Landing 6, 44, 51, 55; Oscan inscription *56*, 59
Etruscan 17, 18, 21, 71
"exedrae" 37, 41, 44, 51n3–n8

Fossa di Papa districts; ancient road and modern road 30
Fratte di Salerno 17

Giannettasio, N.P. 6
Greco, E. 64, 77n19, 79n49
Greece 75
Greek: cities 71, 73; colonisation 64–65; cult of 79n50; literary tradition 65; *pantheon 74*; sanctuaries 1; Surrentum with origins of 3, 18, 21, 82; territories of Taras 74
Gulf of Naples 1, 17, 71

Hegius 62
Hellenistic epoch 83; cave 81n79; head 69–70, *70*, 75; Italic sanctuaries 61
Hera 65, 80n70, 81n77

Irno and Pompeii, mouth of 17

Jacobelli, L. 13, 60
Johannowsky, W. 52, 63n1

kantharoi 74, *75*
kourotrophoi 67, *69*, 74, 82

Li Galli 64
limestone 1, 13, 30, 34, 35, 37, 39, 41, 44, 55, 56, 57, 58, 63n10
Liparus 3, 17, 78n43, 79n50

marble 6, 7, 62, 73
Massa Lubrense 7, 13, *62*; archaeological area of *14*; archaeological storage *67*; Athena Ilias heads *69*; Hellenistic head 70; *kourotrophos* figurines *69*; late archaic heads *67*; Statuette of Athena Ilias *68*
Mele, Alfonso 65, 77n19–n21, 78n45
Mingazzini, P. 3, 8, *9*, 10, 11, 18, 38–39, 44, 51n1–12, 52, 63n3; drawing 35, 37; discussion on the cult 64–65
Morel, J.P. 8, 10, 11, 13, 15n13
mosaics 7
Murat, J. 6, 13, 41, 44, *48*, 55–56

Naples 10, 65
Neapolis 17, 65, 66, 71, 73–74, 78n41–n42, 82, 83n3
necropolis of 16, 18, 20, 21; Hotel Vittoria in Sorrento *66*; Sant'Agata sui Due Golfi *65*, 78n42
nymphai 74, 75, 78n39, 80n69

orthophoto of Punta Campanella 5n1, *54*
Oscan inscription 10, *56*, 59, 62, 82

Pappalardo, U. 6
Parthenope 65, 73, 75, 77n20
Pfister, F. 8, 39, 51n1–n12
Phlegraean fields 1
Piano di Sorrento 6, 21, *24–25*; archaic building detail of *24*; "G. Vallet" *8*, *65*, *68*; 1987–1990 excavations *22*; site plan of 1999–2004 excavations *23*; Via Mortora San Liborio, discovery in 24; Via San Massimo 21, *22–23*
Picentino 17
Pliny the Elder 3, 64
Pompeii 13, 17, 21, 55, 61, 62, 71, 73, 78n41, n42, 83; Triangular Forum in 75–76, 78n49
Portale, E.C. 74, 78n39
Posidonia 66–67, 71, 72, 73, 77n25, 79n52, 82, 83n3
pre-Roman Sorrentine Peninsula 21
Punta Campanella 1, *1*, 30, *57*, 83; ancient structures 4, *53*, *60*; in Angevin period 6; Aragonese, remodelling by 6; archaeological investigations at 8–10; archaeological record *35*; with Capri in background *2*; Coppola A. 10; end of World War II 7–8; excavations 6, 36; first and second terraces,

Index

floor plan *55*; medieval structures 4; Mingazzini, site plan of *9*; modern structures 4; in nineteenth century 6–7; orthophoto of *54*; Oscan inscription on *56*; research 6; in Roman empire 6; sanctuary entrance 36–49, *54*; site plan and floor plans 3–5; Soprintendenza investigations in 1987 *11*, *12*; systematic excavation at 10–11; 3D model of *2*, *3*; *see also* Athena; Sorrentine Peninsula

Rhodes 73, 75–6
road 30, *31–32*, 37, 52; modern *vs.* ancient 13, 27, 33; "mule track" 15n9; paved 8, 24, 30, 33, 36, 59, 63n3, 82
Roman architecture 6, 37, 64, 79n49; building material 7; cave 81n79; inscription *62*; *opus incertum* 37, 39, 41, 51, 58–59; *opus reticulatum* 44; *opus signinum* 37, 39, 40, 41, 51n9, n10
Russo, M. 3, 10, 11, 15n21, 16n24, n27, 65, 66

Samnites 18, 78–79n49, 81n95
San Massimo 21, *22–23*
sanctuary entrance, in Punta Campanella *36–39*, *40*; excavations of 1987 36; first terrace *41–43*; floor plan of 54; fourth terraces *49*; Roman concrete 37; second terrace 44, *45–47*; third terrace *48*, *50*
sanctuary of Athena 10, 52, 64, 71, 74
Sant'Agata sui Due Golfi 18, 65, 78n42; necropolis of *65*
Sarno 17, 18, 20
Sirens: and Athena 64–75, 77n19, 80n68; cult of 3, 17; death of 65; Greek colonization 65; myth of 65; sanctuary of 65–74; sixth century BC 66
Sorrentine Peninsula 1, *1*; archaeological sources 17; boundaries of 27; evolution of 17; fourth century BC 18, 23; fifth century BC 18; necropoleis 18, 19; pre-Roman empire 17–19; primordial kingdoms 17–18; in Roman period 24; sanctuary of 17; sixth century BC 18; seventh century BC 17–18, 23; *see also* Punta Campanella
Stabiae 13, 18, 27, 67, 70, 71, 73, 78n41, 83; in Privati sanctuary 78n49
Statius 3, 62, 64, 81n88
Stephanus of Byzantium 18
structures, in archaeological site 4, *50*, *80*; ancient *53*, *60*; masonry 58; rectangular structures 52; sanctuary of 58; site plan of *53*; on terraces 59; in Via Minervia *39*, 40–41
Surrentum 17, 74, 76, 82; ancient history of 3; archaeological point of view 64–65; cult of Athena 64–65; under Greek influence 82; historical point of view 64–65; pre-Roman period 19–21; Roman era 82; territory of 3, 21, 64

Tabula Peutingeriana 62
Tempio di Cerere 73
templum Minervae 62
terrace, of Punta Campanella 6, 10, 12, 52, *61*; first terrace 36, *41–43*; floor plan of *55*; fourth terrace *49*, 55; second terrace 37, 41, *44*, *45–47*; third terrace 41, 44, *48*, *50*, 55; walls and structures *50*
Tiberius 8, 52
Timaeus of Locri 3
Trinità district 76n14, 77n17; 1987 and 1990 excavations 21, *22*, 24
Tuccinardi, M. 15n20

Ulysses 64, 65, 73, 76, 78–79n49, 78n43

Vesuvius 17, 30
Via Minervia 11, 13, 19, 20, *29*, 33, 35–39, 52, 59, 63n9, n10, 76; ancient road section *31–32*; assays *31–32*; excavation site plan *14*; *opus incertum* section of *27*; polygonal masonry section of *28*; site plan of last route *33*
Via Mortora San Liborio, discovery in 24, *25*

Zancani Montuoro, P. 18, 78n49
Zevi, F. 10

For Product Safety Concerns and Information please contact our EU representative GPSR@taylorandfrancis.com
Taylor & Francis Verlag GmbH, Kaufingerstraße 24, 80331 München, Germany

www.ingramcontent.com/pod-product-compliance
Lightning Source LLC
Chambersburg PA
CBHW051758230426
43670CB00012B/2334